Abortion and Euthanasia

ISSUES FOR THE NINETIES

Volume 4

Editor

Craig Donnellan

Independence

Educational Publishers

First published by Independence
PO Box 295
Cambridge CB1 3XP

British Library Cataloguing in Publication Data
Abortion and Euthanasia – (Issues for the Nineties Series)
I. Donnellan, Craig II. Series
179.7

ISBN 1 872995 58 6

Printed in Great Britain
at Black Bear Press Ltd
Cambridge

Typeset by
Lusher Artwork, Cambridge

Cover
The cartoon on the front cover is by
the artist, Ken Pyne.

CONTENTS

Chapter 1: Abortion

Global overview of abortion	1
Abortions	3
Life or death	4
The NHS and the pro-life hospital	5
Questions you ask about abortion	6
Life	8
Abortion statistics	9
Religious views on abortion	10
Abortion and the law	11
A woman's right to choose?	13
It's murder out there	15
Eight myths about abortion	17
Pre-birth screening	18
Helping parents who discover that their baby is abnormal	19

Chapter 2: Euthanasia

Face up to the euthanasia debate	21
Euthanasia: the dilemma of the decade	22
Euthanasia: the big debate	23
The case for legalisation	24
Human value or the scrap-heap?	25
The need for voluntary euthanasia	26
The relief of pain	28
Dutch watch euthanasia on television	29
I sat holding his hand until he was dead	30
His pain was too much for him to bear	31
The Netherlands guidelines	31
Current legislation	32
Yes, help me to die	33
Scots support mercy killing	34
Relatives keener on euthanasia than patients	35
Relative attitudes	35
'One in four' GPs get pleas for euthanasia	36
Doctor euthanasia survey	36
A flicker of hope	37
Index	38
Additional resources	39
Acknowledgements	40

Introduction

Abortion and Euthanasia is the fourth volume in the series:
Issues For The Nineties. The aim of this series is to offer
up-to-date information about important issues in our
world.

Abortion and Euthanasia examines the current debate
surrounding these sensitive issues. The information comes
from a wide variety of sources and includes:

Government reports and statistics
Newspaper reports and features
Magazine articles and surveys
Literature from lobby groups
and charitable organisations.

It is hoped that, as you read about the many aspects of the
issues explored in this book, you will critically evaluate
the information presented. It is important that you decide
whether you are being presented with facts or opinions.
Does the writer give a biased or an unbiased report? If an
opinion is being expressed, do you agree with the writer?

Abortion and Euthanasia offers a useful starting point for
those who need convenient access to information about
the many issues involved. However, it is only a starting
point. At the back of the book is a list of organisations
which you may want to contact for further information.

*****

Global overview of abortion

From the International Planned Parenthood Federation (IPPF)

In every country around the world women try to terminate their pregnancies, if they are convinced this is the only solution left. An abundance of research data indicate that the decision to do so is largely independent of tradition, religion, legal status of abortion, or medical risks involved. In the past decades, it has been accepted in an increasing number of countries that the need for termination of pregnancy can be greatly reduced through offering good family planning information and services. Several countries show very good results in this respect.

But at the same time, there is rapidly growing recognition that abortion is needed, to a far more limited extent, as a back-up method in cases of contraceptive failure. Therefore, safe medical abortion services have been made available in an increasing number of countries. By 1992 almost two thirds of all women had relatively easy access to such services, but on the other hand one quarter of all women are still forced to seek help from unskilled back-street abortionists. They pay a heavy, sometimes fatal, toll. This overview presents and discusses some of the main universal trends.

Legal status of abortion

There are roughly four types of abortion laws:

1 *Very strict*
Abortion is not allowed on any grounds, or only if the pregnancy poses an immediate threat to the woman's life.

2 *Rather strict*
Only some narrowly defined circumstances justify performing an abortion. Specified grounds are often a threat to the woman's physical or mental health, fetal defects and legal indications (rape or incest).

3 *Rather broad*
Abortion is not only permitted for medical, but also for socio-medical or social reasons. These reasons may include low income, poor housing, young or old age, and having a certain number of children.

4 *On request*
Women have a legal right to decide on the termination of pregnancy. In most cases this right only applies to the first three months of pregnancy, although there are notable exceptions.

Excluding small countries with less than a million inhabitants, there are now 50 countries where the abortion law is very strict, and a further 44 countries where it is rather strict. Thirteen countries have rather broad laws, and in 22 countries women have a legal right to decide for themselves. Most of the latter countries are situated in Europe, whereas in Africa and Latin America very or rather strict abortion laws are still most common.

During the past decades many countries have liberalised their abortion laws. In Japan, abortion has been legal since 1948. During the 1950s abortion was legalised in Eastern Europe, the Soviet Union and China. This trend was followed in the 1960s and 1970s by most Western European countries, the United States and a few other countries. Although it sometimes seemed that this universal trend would be reversed, the worldwide process of liberalisation continued after 1980. In an increasing number of countries women are no longer

Photo: National Abortion Campaign

The abortion issue has generated much debate

forced to seek help from illegal and unskilled abortionists. Table 1 gives an overview of recent legal changes.

It should be emphasised that in countries with restrictive legislation, medically safe abortion services are sometimes readily available and, conversely, in countries where abortion is legally permitted, it may be difficult to find a medical practitioner who is willing to perform an abortion. Quite often safe abortion services are only available to the rich.

Although a majority of countries have very or rather restrictive abortion laws, most women live in countries where abortion is available on request of the woman, or on broadly defined grounds. This is because the most populous countries tend to have liberal laws. In the four largest countries of the world abortion is legal on request (China, the former Soviet Union, and the United States), or on social grounds (India). Most of the smaller countries, in terms of population size, have restrictive laws. As a result, only a quarter of all women in the world do not have any access to legal abortion, and 41 per cent of women have a legal right to decide for themselves.

Global incidence of abortion

Accurate abortion statistics are only available from countries where the procedure is legal. In countries where it is illegal we have to rely on estimates, which are usually based on the number of admissions to hospitals for the treatment of complications caused by illegally or self-induced abortion. Sometimes estimates are based on survey data.

According to the most recent and most reliable estimates, the annual number of induced abortions worldwide is between 36 and 53 million. This number means that, on average, every woman in the world will have one abortion during her lifetime (between 0.9 and 1.3), or each year about 4 per cent of all women in the world have an abortion. Probably, roughly one quarter of all pregnancies worldwide are deliberately terminated. In other words, abortion is very often used to prevent the birth of an unwanted child.

Table 1:
Major changes in the abortion laws 1980–1992

Country	Year	From	To
Netherlands	1981	Very strict	On request
Zambia	1983	Very strict	Rather strict
Turkey	1983	Rather strict	On request
Greece	1986	Rather strict	On request
Czechoslovakia	1986	Rather broad	On request
Canada	1988	Rather strict	On request
Romania	1990	Very strict	On request
Belgium	1990	Very strict	On request
Albania	1992	Very strict	On request
Germany (West)	1992	Rather broad	On request

A popular fallacy maintains that the incidence of abortion is dependent on its legal status: the easier it is to obtain abortion, the more women will use it. But reliable statistics show that in many countries where abortion is legally available the incidence is much lower than in countries where it is completely illegal. For example, in Latin America, where abortion is almost completely illegal, the abortion rate is probably between 30 and 60 per 1,000 women, whereas in Western Europe, where it is legal (except Ireland), the rate is about 14 per 1,000, or two to four times lower.

Legal and safe abortion services do not create their own demand. On the contrary, the need for abortion is primarily an outcome of the availability and quality of family planning services and family planning and sexual education. For example, the poor

> *Although a majority of countries have very or rather restrictive abortion laws, most women live in countries where abortion is available on request of the woman, or on broadly defined grounds*

availability and quality of these services in Russia and other parts of the former Soviet Union are largely responsible for the high abortion rates in those countries. These rates are about 10 times higher than in Western Europe.

Consistent use of contraception greatly reduces the need for abortion, but it cannot completely eliminate this need. This is because most contraceptive methods are not 100 per cent reliable, and users sometimes make mistakes. Therefore, even in countries with very high quality contraceptive services, abortion is needed as a back-up method in cases of contraceptive failure, if only to a limited extent.

The lowest abortion rate currently found (in the Netherlands) is 5 per 1,000 women of fertile age. If this rate were to apply worldwide, there would be fewer than 6 million abortions yearly, instead of the current 36 – 53 million.

Unsafe abortion

According to recent estimates made by the World Health Organization, about one quarter to one third of maternal deaths are due to complications of (illegally) induced abortion. Almost all these 150,000 deaths occur in countries with very strict abortion laws. In other words, repressive abortion legislation does not prevent abortion, it just prevents safe abortion, and turns abortion into a major killer of women.

In countries where abortion is legal, death rates are usually below 1 per 100,000 procedures. The main factors explaining this increasing

safety are;
- Medical doctors, instead of unskilled practitioners, perform the operation.
- Proper facilities and equipment can be used.
- Doctors can be trained in performing the operation.
- Services become better accessible to women, thereby reducing the duration of pregnancy at the time of abortion.
- Proper information can be given to women, which also prevents them from coming late.

In fact, if the proper conditions exist, abortion is a very safe operation. If these conditions were to be met worldwide, the death toll of abortion could be reduced from the current 150,000 to no more than 250 annually, which is 5 per million operations.

Deaths due to clandestine abortions constitute only the tip of the iceberg. Other, often serious complications, such as permanent infertility, are much more prevalent. Treatment of complications of clandestine abortion often poses a heavy burden on the health care system. Particularly in poor countries with scarce medical resources, this may cause insoluble problems. The following problems have been described in the literature:
- up to 40 per cent of admissions to maternity hospitals being due to complications of illegal abortions;
- up to 50 per cent of budgets of maternity hospitals being spent on these treatments;
- bed occupancy rates in maternity wards of up to 300 per cent, largely resulting from abortion complications;
- large shares of scarce blood supplies needed for these treatments;
- heavy, sometimes unbearable burden on medical staff, causing high sick leave.

These and other tragic worldwide consequences of illegal and unskilled abortions can be prevented, firstly, through high quality family planning services and education, and secondly through offering easily accessible, safe abortion services.

- The above is an extract from *Planned Parenthood Challenges* published by IPPF. See page 39 for address details.

© *International Planned Parenthood Federation*

Abortions

Marital status, age and gestation/weeks (residents only)

England and Wales

Year and quarter	All ages				All women						Gestation (weeks)			
	All women	Single women	Married women	Other*	Under 16	16-19	20-34	35-44	45 and over	Age not stated	Under 13	13-19	20 and over	Not stated
Numbers *(thousands)*														
1971	94.6	44.3	41.5	8.7	2.30	18.2	56.0	15.9	0.45	1.80	70.4	20.6	0.85	2.69
1976	101.9	50.9	40.3	10.7	3.43	24.0	57.5	14.7	0.48	1.79	82.1	15.3	0.98	3.56
1981	128.6	70.0	42.4	16.1	3.53	31.4	74.9	17.6	0.56	0.56	108.5	17.4	17.2	1.02
1987	156.2	100.7	38.2	17.3	3.76	35.2	99.5	17.4	0.39	0.01	135.8	18.2	2.22	0.01
1988	168.3	111.0	38.7	18.6	3.57	37.9	108.7	17.7	0.41	0.01	146.0	19.6	2.70	0.01
1989	170.5	113.0	38.1	19.3	3.38	36.2	112.8	17.7	0.39	0.01	149.8	18.3	2.40	0.01
1990	173.9	116.2	38.2	19.6	3.42	35.2	116.5	18.1	0.40	0.01	152.7	19.0	2.26	0.01
1991	167.4	110.9	37.8	18.7	3.16	31.1	114.7	17.9	0.41	0.01	147.5	17.8	2.07	0.00
1992	160.5	105.6	36.4	18.5	3.00	27.6	111.4	18.1	0.45	0.01	142.2	16.5	1.86	0.00
1989 March	42.4	28.3	9.52	4.64	0.91	9.12	28.0	4.32	0.10	0.00	37.4	4.97	0.67	0.00
June	42.7	28.3	9.50	4.87	0.81	9.06	28.3	443	0.09	0.00	38.1	4.63	0.66	0.00
Sept	41.9	27.8	9.42	4.75	0.80	8.70	27.9	4.40	0.10	0.00	36.9	4.50	0.57	0.00
Dec	41.3	27.4	9.12	4.80	0.79	8.81	27.3	4.31	0.09	0.00	36.7	4.10	0.50	0.00
1990 March	44.9	30.1	9.59	5.24	0.87	9.30	30.1	4.56	0.10	0.00	39.1	5.21	0.63	0.00
June	42.4	28.1	9.33	4.95	0.75	8.50	28.6	4.48	0.09	0.00	37.3	4.51	0.58	0.00
Sept	42.3	28.5	9.28	4.53	0.83	8.84	28.2	4.36	0.09	0.00	37.1	4.72	0.55	0.00
Dec	41.9	28.0	9.34	4.62	0.86	8.36	28.2	4.38	0.10	0.00	37.2	4.32	0.48	0.00
1991 March	44.7	29.9	9.85	4.89	0.80	8.84	30.3	4.65	0.11	0.01	38.9	5.14	0.59	0.00
June	40.9	27.2	9.18	4.60	0.72	7.43	28.3	4.41	0.08	0.01	36.0	4.37	0.54	0.00
Sept	40.6	26.8	9.25	4.51	0.79	7.42	27.8	4.44	0.11	0.00	35.9	4.20	0.46	0.00
Dec	39.3	25.8	9.06	4.48	0.77	7.06	27.2	4.23	0.10	0.00	35.0	3.86	0.44	0.00
1992 March	41.8	27.9	9.16	4.72	0.79	7.44	28.9	4.55	0.12	0.00	36.5	4.76	0.49	0.00
June	39.4	25.8	8.94	4.57	0.64	6.72	27.5	4.37	0.11	0.00	34.7	3.41	0.47	0.00
Sept	39.4	25.9	8.95	4.54	0.74	6.88	27.1	4.51	0.11	0.00	34.9	3.99	0.47	0.00
Dec	38.6	25.1	8.95	4.50	0.76	6.29	26.9	4.50	0.11	0.00	34.7	3.41	0.42	0.00
1993 March	41.7	27.4	9.38	4.91	0.76	7.05	28.9	4.90	0.13	0.00	36.9	4.30	0.50	0.00
June	38.0	25.1	8.42	4.51	0.74	6.08	26.5	4.60	0.12	0.00	33.7	3.94	0.44	0.00

© OPCS
Winter, 1994

Life or death

From the Society for the Protection of the Unborn Child (SPUC)

Photo: Joanne O'Brien/Format

What are we to think of a woman who aborts her child?
Let's be very clear. We understand the agony of her decision. We want to stand with her, not against her. We want to help her explore other loving alternatives like adoption. We want to help her. Why can't we love them both?

But adopted children have serious problems.
Not so at all. Compared, across the board, to children born into families, adopted children are more stable, more healthy, more educated and lead more stable lives as adults, than biological children – they are, that is, if placed in the adoptive home as young infants. These problems are not from adoption; however. Rather they bring the problems with them and sometimes the adoptive parents are unable to cope with them.

But isn't it cruel to allow a handicapped child to be born to a miserable life?
The assumption that handicapped people enjoy life less than 'normal' ones has been shown to be false. A well documented investigation has shown that there is no difference between handicapped and normal persons in their degree of life satisfaction, outlook of what lies immediately ahead and vulnerability to frustration. 'Though it may be both common and fashionable to believe that the malformed enjoy life less than normal, this appears to lack both empirical and theoretical support.' Paul Cameron & D Van Hoeck, Am. Psychologic Association meeting, 1971.

What about a woman who's been raped?
Pregnancy from forcible rape is extremely rare. The victim must be supported, loved and helped, but we should never kill an innocent baby for the crime of his father.

But legal abortion is better than dangerous back-alley abortions and their toll of women dying, isn't it?
Most such stories are false. In 1972, the year before the US Supreme Court decision on abortion, only 39 women died in all 50 states from illegal abortions. (25 more died in 1972 from legal abortions). These were 39 tragedies, but compared to over 5,000,000 pregnancies that year this is a minuscule number. Certainly it shows that claims of 5–10,000 deaths and one million illegal abortions are totally ridiculous.

Either there were not many illegal abortions or all illegal abortions were amazingly safe.

What about her right to choose?
The first question to ask about any action that is morally questionable is not 'Who can choose to do it?' but 'Is the action right or wrong in the first place?' Consider other examples such as rape, stealing, child abuse. Do we first ask who decides, who can choose to do these things? No! We first ask

'Are these actions right or wrong?' Just so with abortion. The first question must be 'Is abortion right or wrong?' The 'choice and who decides?' question follows. It is never the first question.

Another answer to 'choice' is, choice to do what? Clearly it is a choice to kill.

Isn't abortion another means of contraception?
No. Do not confuse abortion with contraception. Contraception prevents new life from beginning. Abortion kills the new life that has already begun.

What is an abortifacient then?
Some of today's so-called 'contraceptives' are really abortive at times. This is when ovulation is not suppressed, fertilisation does occur, but the one week old living human embryo is unable to implant into the wall of her womb. If the 'contraceptive' drug or device prevents implantation then it is really an abortifacient.

I've heard abortion compared to slavery.

The analogy is accurate. The Dred Scott Decision in 1857 ruled that black people were not 'persons' in the eyes of the Constitution. Slaves could be bought, sold, used or even killed as property of the owner. That decision was overturned by the 14th Amendment. Now the Court has ruled that unborn people are not 'persons' in the eyes of the Constitution. They can be killed at the request of their owners (mothers). This dreadful decision can only be reversed by the Court itself or overturned by another constitutional amendment.

Why bring unwanted babies into the world?

An unwanted pregnancy in the early months does not necessarily mean an unwanted baby after delivery. Dr Edward Lenoski (University of South California) has conclusively shown that 90% of battered children were planned pregnancies. Since when does someone's life depend upon someone else wanting them? That is an incredibly evil ethic.

Abortion is only a religious question, isn't it?

No. Theology certainly concerns itself with respect for human life. It must turn to science, however, to tell it when life begins. The question of abortion is a basic human question that concerns the entire civilised society in which we live. It is not just a Catholic, or Protestant, or Jewish issue. It is a civil rights question, a human rights question, a question of who lives and who can be killed.

A civil rights question? How so?

1) The first question is to be asked is: What is this inside of her womb? Is it a human life? The answer is found in natural science, medicine and biology. At the first cell stage, fertilisation, this being is alive, not dead. Human? Yes, not another species. Sexed? Yes, male or female from fertilisation. Complete? Yes, nothing has been added to the single cell, whom each of us once was, nothing except nutrition and oxygen.

Science has long since shown conclusively that this is a human life from the beginning.

2) The second question is: Should there be equal protection by law for all living humans, or should the law discriminate, fatally against an entire class of living humans as with abortion, which discriminates on the basis of age (too young) and place of residence (living in the womb). So, abortion is a violation of human rights, of civil rights.

What about emotional after-effects?

Some women have problems soon after the abortion. The big problem, however, is usually many years later. This is now called 'Post-Abortion Syndrome'. By virtue of suppression and denial, such women repress any negative feelings for, on average, at least five years. Then, a variety of symptoms emerge, many of which can be very upsetting and even disabling. It is similar to the post-traumatic stress syndrome seen a decade or more later in some combat veterans.

There is treatment for this but many doctors do not know how. If a woman is troubled, she should seek a referral from a pro-life pregnancy help centre.

• Reprinted with permission from Hayes Publishing Co and the authors Dr. & Mrs. J.C Wilke.

The NHS and the pro-life hospital

By George Makin

Life, Britain's largest anti-abortion group, plans to use NHS cash to fund a 'pro-life' hospital. The first stage is the opening of a medical centre on the site of a former convent in Liverpool next month. The organisation aims to sell services to GP fund-holders to create income for its long-term objective of building a hospital based on pro-life principles. This means it would not carry out terminations or treatments such as IVF.

Anna Furedi of the Birth Control Trust voices the fears of pro-choice groups: 'We would be extremely concerned if any NHS funding were to go to such a centre. Women requiring treatment should have the full range of services available.'

Nuala Scarisbrick, Life's press officer, has said: 'The centre will offer a range of healthcare facilities for safe pregnancies and healthy families' but other statements have landed her in trouble with the Liverpool Health Authority, which has complained about press releases outlining medical services for which the centre is not registered. These included infertility treatment and a hospice for new-born babies with disabilities.

The centre is the first concrete example of the change in Life's strategy after its disastrous attempt in 1990 to amend the 1967 Abortion Act. In the aftermath Life determined to switch from political lobbying to social provision.

Questions you ask about abortion

Is abortion murder? Are women having abortions being selfish? Are abortions on grounds of disability wrong? These are just a few of the questions that the National Abortion Campaign (NAC) gets asked every day by people studying the rights and wrongs of abortion

Introduction

NAC came into existence in 1975 and very soon afterwards we started to get students and others writing to us asking for our views on various aspects of abortion. This article is based on over 15 years of answering queries about our views.

Every time a woman is pregnant and is not sure whether or not she wants to have a baby, she has to make up her mind what she is going to do. Whatever her decision, the chances are that it can never be 100% satisfactory – like most things in real life. What women and those trying to help them attempt to do is to ensure the best outcome in each particular case. Understanding the issues involved can help you prepare for making similar decisions, or in helping friends trying to make such difficult decisions, or simply in shaping your attitudes towards women who have faced this dilemma.

Is abortion murder?

Abortion can only be thought of as 'murder' if you believe that the fetus is a person. And even if you believe that it may be a person, with the same rights as the mother, abortion can be viewed as self-defence on the part of the woman who decides to have an abortion – she does so because she believes that the pregnancy threatens her in some way.

Even before abortion was made legal under certain circumstances, it was not legally murder and was treated differently under the law.

People have different views about the 'personhood' of the fetus. Politicians, religious leaders, doctors,

By Leonora Lloyd and Mandy Coates

scientists and philosophers have never been able to agree. There is no 'right' answer. Sometimes, anti-abortionists argue that, therefore, we should give the 'benefit of the doubt' to the fetus and assume that it is a person.

The problem with this argument is, first, that this will not prevent women having 'back-street abortions' – and these are likely to be dangerous and may be life-threatening – and, second, it assumes that we are prepared to impose our beliefs (or, in this case, doubts) on others, however strongly they disagree with us. So at the end of the day, it must be the individual's choice.

Of course the fetus is alive, and it could develop into a human being, but research shows that about 50 – 70% of all conceptions end in early miscarriage, often even before the woman is aware that she is pregnant. Clearly, the fetus is a potential human being, not an actual one.

Many women who have abortions have mixed feelings about what they are doing. It is seldom an easy decision and for some women it is a fact that under different circumstances they would not have the abortion. Sometimes women may regret having had an abortion, and sometimes women who decide not to have an abortion regret that decision too.

Doesn't the fetus / baby have any rights?

Of course it does. It has the right to be born wanted. There is ample evidence that throughout history women have tried to control the number of children they have and when they have them, through using contraception and abortion, often at great risk to their own lives and health. They know that if they are to be able to look after their children properly, they must control the number they have, both from the point of view of their own health and the resources they have – their income, housing, etc. Often it is only because of pressure from men in their society and family – who may want them to have more children, especially boys – that women have as many children as they do. A survey by the World Health Organization showed that in many parts of the world women want smaller families than is the custom for their society.

Some research has been done into what happens to children who are born unwanted. In this country, like many where abortion is legal, a great many statistics are kept about women who have abortions, but none at all about those whose request is refused, so we don't know how many of them there are and how many go on to have babies, or what happens to those babies. In Sweden before the second world war abortion was legal, but women had to go before hospital boards and plead their case, so there were records of women who were turned down. Some of them went on to have illegal abortions, but a study was made of a group of women who continued with their pregnancies after being refused abortion, and they, their families, and the children born as a result were compared to a similar group of women who had not sought abortion. It was found that the children born after their mothers had been refused an abortion generally did worse on every count – education, jobs, even their marriages did not last as long! And this disadvantage extended to their families, because their parents' marriage was also more likely to break up. Boys in particular were more likely to die in their teens or early twenties. A later study done in Yugoslavia found similar results.

Recent research into children who are adopted or taken into care shows that many of them have par-ticular problems as well; children in care in this country are likely to have many foster families or end up going from one institution to another. Many of the homeless young people causing concern at the moment have been in care or have been fostered.

In considering whether or not to have an abortion, most women take the quality of life of their future child into consideration. For each woman, in each society, this will be different, but throughout the world women want the best for their children. For most women, they think of this as a basic right for any children they may have, and this is why they try so hard to plan their families.

But isn't it better to have been born than not to be?

This is really a nonsense question. If you haven't been born, you don't know you might have been born, do you? In any case, even many of those who have been born wish they had not, and take their own lives – including many very young people.

This question is asked by anti-abortionists to make us feel insecure, but in fact your existence – as YOU – is not dependant simply on the fact that your mother decided not to abort you, but on all sorts of factors which

Photo: National Abortion Campaign

determined which particular egg from your mother met a particular sperm from your father – and of course, THEIR existence depended on similar factors, right back to the start of the human race. Throughout that time, women have used abortion to control the size of their families, but you still got born, as did many billions of others, good, bad, famous, unknown, those who lived to be a hundred and those who barely drew breath before dying.

Don't handicapped babies have the right to live?

The National Abortion Campaign does not believe that the fact that a baby may be born with a disability, however severe, is in itself a ground for abortion. In fact, we believe there should be only one ground – that the woman does not want to continue with her pregnancy. Her reasons are her own business, but the fact is that some women (less than one out of every hundred having an abortion) do so because of a diagnosis of disability in their expected baby.

This diagnosis is made as a result of various tests during the pregnancy. Women have the right to refuse to take the tests and even if they decide

to have them and it turns out that they are very probably carrying a baby with a disability, they should not be pressured into have an abortion – it must be their decision. Every woman is different and she alone knows what she and her family can cope with. She may already have a child or other relative with a similar handicap if it is hereditary, and so she knows what to expect. If she already has a child with a disability, she may feel that both children suffer if she has to take care of a second baby with the same problem. In some cases, the disability may be so severe that the baby may be born dead or be very likely to die at or shortly after birth.

Women who decide to continue with their preg-nancies despite knowing that they will have a baby with a disability have the right to all the support they need, and this does not include being told that they have no right to give birth to such a baby and that they should have had an abortion. Women who are themselves disabled have the right to have babies and all disabled people have the right to a full life.

There is no evidence that countries where abortion is illegal take better care of their disabled citizens – quite the opposite if anything. Sweden, for example, has a very liberal abortion law, but it also has much better laws and practice on rights for disabled people than most other countries. In Romania, when abortion was completely illegal, mentally and physically handicapped children and adults were shut up in the most disgusting conditions, and no resources were devoted to caring for them or to their education.

● The above is an extract from *Questions you ask about abortion*. published by the National Abortion Campaign. See page 39 for address details.

may be performed if the requirements of the Abortion Act are fulfilled, but not otherwise.

The Secretary of State for Health may approve classes of places outside NHS or NHS Trust hospitals, as opposed to individual places, for the purpose of treatment for the termination of pregnancy which consists primarily of using abortifacient drugs (specified when approval is given).

The law does not apply to Northern Ireland.

What the law means

It is illegal – against the law – to have an abortion in this country unless two doctors agree that the woman can have one. The doctors must both fill in forms showing the reasons – grounds – why they are agreeing that the woman can have the abortion. Abortions can only be done by doctors and they must be done either in an NHS or NHS Trust hospital or in a private clinic or hospital specially registered by the Department of Health. Under regulations applied by the Department, only clinics having special licences can do abortions using RU486 and another special licence is needed to do abortions after 20 weeks. After 24 weeks, only NHS and NHS Trust hospitals can do abortions (except in emergencies, to save the woman's life, when they can be performed by any medical practitioner).

There is no right in law for a woman to have an abortion. She must have those two doctors' permission, and they must satisfy themselves that at least one of the grounds laid down in the law applies. Abortion is the only medical procedure for which this is necessary.

In most cases, the woman must be under 24 weeks pregnant at the time of the abortion. Only when the doctors are sure there is a serious risk to the woman's life, or mental or physical health, or that the baby, if born, would suffer from serious abnormalities, can an abortion be done later than 24 weeks.

The grounds (reasons) for abortion include the effect of the pregnancy on the woman's mental or physical health, the health of any children she already has, or fetal

Campaigning for choice

abnormality (handicap). It does not specifically include the pregnancy being the result of rape or incest.

If the woman's life is in danger, or if her health would suffer permanently as a result of the pregnancy, then one doctor can agree to terminate the pregnancy, as an emergency, at anytime during the pregnancy. After the stage at which the baby might be born alive, the doctor should also try to save the baby's life, but his/her first duty is to the woman.

The Secretary of State for Health can decide, without having to go back to Parliament, that places other than NHS and NHS Trust hospitals and licensed private clinics can do abortions. This would apply if she or he decided that it was safe to allow places like family planning clinics or even General Practitioners to perform abortions using RU486 or at least to use the first stage of this method.

The law does not apply to Northern Ireland.

Important note

Although abortions can only be done with permission of a doctor, they are also against the law if done without the permission of the woman concerned, unless she is unable to give consent (for example, when she is in a coma) and the doctor considers it necessary to save her life. However, even in these circumstances, the doctor must attempt to contact her nearest relative and obtain permission.

In the case of under sixteen year olds, permission is also required from a parent or guardian. When the girl and her parents disagree, the courts must make the decision and in recent cases, they have taken the side of the girl, whether she wanted an abortion against her parents' wishes or the opposite way round. In cases where the woman, although of age, is considered mentally incompetent to make a reasoned decision herself the courts will again decide, taking into account the wishes of the woman as far as possible, together with the wishes of those looking after her, as well as advice from doctors and social workers.

• The above is an extract from *Abortion Facts and Figures* published by the National Abortion Council. See page 39 for address details.

© National Abortion Campaign
January, 1994

A woman's right to choose?

Women and the problem pregnancy

We all know what abortion does to the unborn child. But there's one other very important person involved. The woman. What happens to her?

What we are told

For over 25 years women in Britain have been told that abortion was a safe little procedure, involving no big problems. Women needed abortion to have total control over their fertility and total freedom to choose what to do with their lives. Abortion would bring with it a new status for women. At last women would be equal with men because they would not have to bear unwanted children. So we were told.

Safe little procedure?

Abortion is invasive of women's bodies whatever method is used, whether surgical or chemical. Surgical methods can damage future fertility as well as cause immediate infection. Chemical abortion uses drugs that are immediately dangerous for some women, painful to use, and can have still uncharted long-term effects on women's health.

After abortion women are more likely to miscarry or give birth prematurely.

No big problems ?

Abortion causes more than physical damage to women. Abortion abuses women. It leaves many women filled with anger, guilt, regret, loss of self-esteem, and unable to trust others. Relationships often collapse after abortion, and many women are left with no man, no baby, and alienated parents. No one forgets an abortion.

For some women the strain of coping, often alone, with their feelings afterwards causes more problems than any posed by the unwanted pregnancy.

Total control over their fertility?

The amount of unplanned pregnancy has risen steadily since abortion was legalised. This is despite free contraception for everyone, even under-age girls, since 1974. So what's happened to fertility control?

Readily available abortion means that, if conception occurs, the problem can be 'solved' at once. Inevitably there is more sexual activity at ever younger ages. No contraception, much of which is anyway abortifacient, is totally effective. So there are more and more unplanned pregnancies.

Freedom to choose?

When pregnancy is unwanted what real choice is there?

The choice is between abortion, with its physical and emotional after-effects, or continuing the pregnancy.

Those people closely involved with the pregnant woman know that if pregnancy continues they will be expected to do something to help her and her baby. If she has an abortion they need do nothing. She has the abortion alone. She has to live with it afterwards – alone.

For selfish partners, parents, friends, the choice is simple. They do the choosing, not her. Sometimes the pressure is gentle. Often it isn't. There is little freedom of choice when those who should give love and support walk away leaving her to cope alone. Readily available abortion has made women more vulnerable.

Control over their lives?

Pregnancy changes a woman's life, whether or not it ends in abortion. It is possible to plan ahead when continuing pregnancy, and the problems and joys of motherhood can be foreseen. But abortion is a journey into the unknown. No one knows what she will feel like afterwards, either immediately or in the future. Many women are unprepared for the destructive effects of abortion on their lives.

Status of women

But, say the abortionists, it's necessary for the equal status of women that there is safe, legal abortion. Unless women can enjoy the same access to hassle-free sex that men, allegedly, have traditionally enjoyed for centuries, they will never be equal, never have the same chances as men.

Well, in Great Britain women have had 25 years of this chance of achieving equal status. What's happened?

A third of births are now to women who are not married. That may include women in a stable relationship who choose not to marry and have the full support of their partner in childrearing. But it undoubtedly includes many lone mothers who chose against abortion and find they have to cope alone.

Instead of the women enjoying the sexual freedom allegedly conferred by abortion it seems to be exactly what uncaring men like. If the man doesn't want to be involved he just says, 'It's your choice', and pushes off. Some women will then have an abortion but many won't because they know what abortion can do to them, and they appreciate the rights of the child.

A new underclass

These brave women often find that, apart from LIFE, not a lot of people are interested in helping them. The new poor in Britain include many lone mothers with young babies. Are they liberated? Is their status as mothers, as women, appreciated? No. Instead, they are criticised by Government and media pundits as a burden on society.

The enormous rise in divorce has damaged the status of many women. No one asks what the connection is between abortion and divorce. Why not? If most unmarried relationships break up after abortion, won't abortion also damage marriage? One third of women having abortions are married. One third of marriages end in divorce in Britain. Are the two facts connected?

New role-models

The status of women in their unique role as mothers and homemakers has never been so low. All the skills

A LIFE house in Bath

women were traditionally praised for and proud of – connected with family care and home-making – are officially rubbished by the abortion-driven propagandists. Female role-models we are invited to admire usually include women who support abortion, reject children or cannot sustain a relationship.

And where is the enhanced status of women in the visual arts, media, literature? There has never been more violence and pornography directed at and involving women – as well as children. What is the connection between abortion and the way in which women are routinely portrayed even on prime-time television – the rapes, the beatings, the foul language, the sheer vulgarity?

Violence

Abortion itself violates women. And the message that violence is acceptable to women has bred dangerously.

Easy abortion makes women's bodies finally available for sex, with (apparently) no fear of the consequences, and the approval of the chattering classes. So what's wrong in taking the violence and disposability ever further?

The truly pro-woman way

LIFE has for over 20 years counselled and helped hundreds of thousands of women and their families with the problems caused by unwanted pregnancy or abortion. Most members of LIFE are women, with extensive experience of the fears, wishes, hopes of women. LIFE knows that abortion 'solves' nothing, usually leaves women in the same difficult situation as before, and often does such damage to the health of women that they are worse off than ever.

LIFE's free, confidential care for women provides a better way forward in even the most difficult situation: even where pregnancy results from rape, incest or abuse, or the unborn child has been diagnosed as disabled.

LIFE gives help that accepts and respects women and their babies.

© LIFE
February, 1995

It's murder out there

Last month two abortion clinic receptionists were shot dead in Boston. Could pro-life extremists here follow suit? Mary Hampshire measures the current climate

As cars draw in to Fairfield Clinic every 20 minutes or so, there is a disapproving wag of the finger, a shaking of the head and calls of 'Do you know your baby actually moves at seven weeks?' 'Do you know the baby's heart starts beating at twenty weeks?' or pleas of 'We can help you.' A freezing winter chill fails to temper the zealous spirit of protesters outside the Marie Stopes abortion centre at Buckhurst Hill, North London.

They visit twice a week from 7am to 10am carrying rosaries and posters of Our Lady of Guadalupe, the patroness of life and conception according to the Catholic Church.

A guard stands watch to escort women inside. It is a matter of routine since the clinic was targeted by the militant anti-abortion organisation Rescue America two years ago.

Individuals belonging to this group have been implicated in arson and acid attacks, bombings and assaults on staff at clinics across the States. But the most extreme form of protest against abortion in America has been the murder of five people, including two surgeons, during the last two years. In the most recent case last month, a gunman talked his way into a Boston clinic and opened fire with a semi-automatic rifle killing two receptionists.

As a result of this kind of threat, abortion surgeons in America wear bullet-proof vests.

While the general consensus is that British abortion personnel are safer than their American counterparts because of much stricter gun controls, the mimicking of other forms of 'direct action' has forced clinics in London and the regions to review their security measures.

Ann Furedi, deputy director of the Birth Control Trust, explains: 'There has been a fragmentation of the anti-abortion movement and there are a very small number of people who have become very militant.

'We are worried about some of these individuals, even though they represent a tiny minority,' she admits.

'The have picked up ideas from what's been going on in the States. Then we've started to see things happen here a year later.

'I can't say violence is ever justifiable in this context. A dead doctor doesn't guarantee a live baby . . .'

Father James Morrow on the recent shootings in the States

'Some have tried to chain themselves to equipment in waiting rooms. They shout Bible slogans and try to counsel women – we call it harassment.' Josie Blair, spokeswoman for the British Pregnancy Advisory Service, remembers one of the very first instances of direct action at their Liverpool clinic three years ago.

'There was a barrier of people in between the entrance to the clinic and the driveway. Staff were put into a police van for safety but the protesters tried to rock the van.

'They also noted car registration numbers and took videos. The unspoken threat was there. If you can imagine that, for a young person being filmed and not knowing where it's [the film] going to end up was absolutely frightening.' Elsewhere in the country, protesters held banners with the picture of a gynaecologist and his address and home telephone number in the form of a 'wanted' poster at a clinic in Manchester.

Acid was poured over staff cars at a clinic in Brighton recently and a bomb scare meant people being evacuated while operations were carried out.

Ms Furedi of the Birth Control Trust adds: 'They can cause a great deal of distress. You never quite know what they might do next. They are a

problem because they are so unpredictable and largely unstable.' Fairfield Clinic is used to peaceful vigils on a weekly basis, but the staff had to call the police in three years ago when activists broke into an operating theatre inside their premises. That particular demonstration was organised by Rescue UK, set up in 1989 as a British off-shoot of Rescue America. In their attempts to 'rescue' unborn children, they advocate pavement counselling and human blockades. While simultaneously advocating 'peaceful intervention', the organisation has stated: 'Some people may go inside the abortuary where they can continue to pray, to counsel, to educate. Some may physically expose their body between the executioner and his victim.' One of their main figureheads Father James Morrow, a Catholic priest, has been arrested on several occasions in Britain for public order offences. This includes being convicted of assaulting a clinic manager, who was pregnant at the time, which he continues to deny.

He says: 'We draw the line at violence. Protest which is reasonable is standing at gates and doorways in organised sit-ins. We stay there until we are removed.

But he points out: 'If people can get into a clinic to disarm the murderers in order to save a baby then that is perfectly acceptable.

'We have to look at our own country and see that they're killing, quite deliberately, 500 babies every day – that's the real horror.' 'Disarming the murderers,' according to Father Morrow, means wrecking equipment in theatres. He admits to smashing a glass bottle which he says was used to hold the remains of aborted foetuses during the break-in at Fairfield Clinic. At the time no operations were taking place.

Commenting on the recent shootings in the States he adds: 'I can't say violence is ever justifiable in this context. A dead doctor doesn't guarantee a live baby.' Meanwhile, other pro-life pressure groups, such as LIFE, publicly disassociate themselves from fringe activity.

'We are mainly embarrassed by them because we all get lumped together and that doesn't do us the world of good, especially when we're a struggling charity with low funding.

'We see ourselves as the people in between the two extremes,' said senior care officer Josephine Quintavalle.

'I can see how people become frustrated. Because if you consider that abortion is the destruction of human life and you can't do anything about it, you can understand the mentality of wanting to get in there and do something.' On the other side of the fence are the pro-choice lobbyists who have altered their tactics at demonstrations in response to militant protests.

'I do not agree with shooting abortion doctors. If you believe in heaven and hell... I feel they will go straight to hell.'

Fairfield Clinic protester

'We take a different view now. These days we try to be more passive-assertive,' explains Emma Gibson, from the National Abortion Campaign.

'That means no shouting, keeping very calm and no banners or placards. We wear bibs and we are there to help escort the women into a clinic.

'Because,' she adds, 'if everybody is making a lot of noise, the women can't actually tell the difference between the pro-lifers and pro-choicers.' Ms Gibson enrolled on a clinic defence training course in New York where she was briefed in the techniques used by pro-life extremists to disrupt clinics. This includes fainting near a main doorway, pretending to be a pro-abortionist, chaining themselves to equipment and the theft of medical records.

'We feel relatively prepared. We have people who we can call at short notice to go and defend a clinic if need by,' she says.

Differences in social and political culture lead some British abortion providers to believe they will never experience the same intensity of protest that has wreaked havoc on clinics in the States.

Liz Davies, manager of Fairfield Clinic, admits there are occupational hazards but regards it as highly unlikely that their surgeons will ever be required to wear bullet-proof vests.

'I'm not saying it would never ever happen here but I can't see the same violence being tolerated in this country. There isn't such a strong Bible belt in Britain and there is far more rigid gun control.

'And in the States, the anti-abortion lobby has been supported at Government level by the Reagan and Bush administrations.' When the national director of Rescue America, Don Treshman, came to London in 1993 to plan a mass offensive against clinics, he was arrested and released on bail. The condition was that he did not involve himself in any actions which might lead to violence or public disorder, proving the British Government's willingness to intervene.

Says Josie Blair of BPAS: 'At least the Home Office recognised that they didn't want to import this kind of problem to Britain. This kind of action is very alien to our culture.' Back at the Fairfield Clinic, 61 year old Michael stands outside during his weekly vigil armed with leaflets, including some gruesome pictures of aborted foetuses.

His other weapon is a poster of an unborn child proclaiming 'We've abolished the death penalty for murderers and terrorists; shouldn't we abolish it for him too?' In between praying for the staff, women and the postman who delivers mail that morning, he explains: 'I have never been involved in any civil disobedience and would not engage in any kind of violence.

'I do not agree with shooting abortion doctors. If you believe in heaven and hell . . . I feel that they will go straight to hell.' But for abortion providers the future is less clear cut. Because, as Josie Blair cautiously adds: 'We do our best to protect staff . . . but we are not that naive. There is a chance that it could get worse and if it does, it will be through the influence of activists abroad.'

© Ms London
January, 1995

Eight myths about abortion

From the National Abortion Campaign

Abortion only happens to other people

Four out of ten women have had or will have an abortion at some time in this country, according to government statistics.

Abortion is available on demand

You need the permission of two doctors before you can have an abortion, unlike most countries in Europe where it is available on request.

Abortion is dangerous

You are over seven times more likely to die as a result of full-term pregnancy than from a termination. Legal abortion is one of the safest operations available, with a death rate of one in every 100,000 – 200,000 procedures, and a morbidity rate of between 3 and 10 percent.

There are too many abortions

The abortion rate in Britain is lower than in many other countries. Around 13 women in every 1,000 have an abortion every year. It is calculated that, in countries without legal abortion, the rates are generally higher.

There are too many late abortions

In 1991, 2.5 percent of abortions were done after 20 weeks. These terminations can only be done for very serious reasons.

The law makes abortion too easy

Making abortion harder to get does not reduce the numbers. In 1990, the law was changed and made very slightly more liberal. In 1991, numbers fell by 4 percent compared with 1990.

There are no problems and no need to campaign to keep abortion legal

Anti-abortionists are constantly attempting to change the law – some 16 times since the 1967 Act was passed. Without campaigning by the National Abortion Campaign and our sister organisations, we might not have even the inadequate law we do have. But it is not just from Parliament that the dangers come. Anti-abortion groups have tremendous resources which they use to try and persuade women that abortion is dangerous and traumatic – despite all the mass of research evidence to the contrary – thus helping to create needless stress and worry to women seeking to end unwanted pregnancies. Some extremists go further, harassing women and clinic staff outside clinics or even invading clinics. The fact is that we need constant vigilance if abortion rights are to be maintained and improved.

Pro-choice campaigners are in it for the money

Over half of the abortions done on the NHS and most of the rest are done in clinics run by non-profit making charities. Compared to most private medicine, non-NHS abortions are not expensive. None of the organisations actively campaigning for improvements in the law and in provision are funded other than by their members and supporters, most of whom are women, who on average earn much less than men and certainly are not rich. The National Abortion Campaign, like the other groups, is run on a shoestring.

That is why, if you are pro-choice, your active support is so necessary. By joining NAC, you help to ensure that it is able to carry on campaigning to defend and improve abortion law and defend and improve women's access to abortion facilities.

© National Abortion Campaign
November, 1994

Pre-birth screening

Something wrong with baby?

Every pregnant woman is nowadays encouraged, as a matter of routine, to have pre-natal diagnostic tests. When these are done to protect the pregnancy and for the welfare of the unborn child, such procedures are obviously welcome. But in the great majority of cases the real reason is to check for any abnormality of the child and to offer abortion as quickly as possible.

If the child is thought to be disabled, the pressures on the mother to have an abortion will often be very great. In some hospitals women will have been required to agree to abortion in advance – if the tests prove positive. In many places, women are not told clearly what the tests are for, and parents are unprepared for the shock of learning that there is something wrong and being given only a day or so to decide for or against abortion. Few hospitals provide any real counselling to help parents cope with the dis-appointment and heartbreak. They will be hassled into agreeing to a 'termination'.

Parents are rarely told that

a) Pre-natal testing can be seriously inaccurate. It can produce false positives and false negatives. So perfectly healthy children are needlessly killed; many disabled ones are not 'spotted'.
b) Pre-natal testing can cause miscarriage and damage the child seriously.
c) Pre-natal testing may discover a disability but cannot always predict the degree of disability that the child will eventually suffer. So, for instance, the spina bifida detected in the womb may turn out to be a minor abnormality after birth.

d) The law states that eugenic abortion is unlawful unless there is a *substantial* risk of *serious* abnormality of the child.

What's wrong with eugenic abortion ?

First of all, abortion is never easy to handle. LIFE has extensive experience of the effects on women of

Photo: LIFE

A co-founder of Life prepares to open a new LIFE baby shop

abortion and knows that even when abortion seemed to be in the best interests of everyone, the subsequent grief, guilt, alienation and loss of self-esteem can cause long-term trauma to both parents.

In the case of eugenic abortion the trauma may be even more intense because the child would usually have been wanted and the bonding between mother and baby well advanced.

Couples have phoned LIFE's national hotline in anguish because they have been told there's a chance, or a virtual certainty, that there is something wrong with their baby and given the weekend to decide.

The decision is a cold-blooded one. If the parents decide for abortion they have to live forever with the terrible, lingering doubt – was the baby really so abnormal, could they have coped, was it right to deny the child life?

This kind of choice can cause relationship tensions between the parents that may worsen after abortion.

One woman, phoned LIFE after the abortion of a Down's Syndrome child, distressed especially because a neighbouring family have a Down's child whom they love and who seems to live a happy life. The caller was reproaching herself and her husband for not having taken the decision to continue pregnancy.

Most people who ring LIFE say that they have had little positive help at the hospital, and, indeed, have been given the result of the tests in an abrupt and hurtful way. Few of them have been told about the help that is available from the many specialist charities for dis-abled people.

They have met only negative and defeatist attitudes.

It is not surprising that, in their despair and hurt, most couples have an abortion and then have to pick up the pieces of their lives alone – unless they find LIFE.

Right to life of disabled people

Public attitudes to disability are strangely confused. Before birth the disabled person is officially worthless – to be hunted down by pre-natal diagnostic tests and aborted.

After birth the law gives equal protection and equal opportunity to disabled people: public buildings have to have access and lavatory facilities for wheelchairs; large businesses are expected to employ a percentage of disabled people; 'normal' schools are expected to provide education for all but seriously disabled children. After birth disabled people have a chance of fair treatment and equal rights.

But if the policy is to destroy more and more of them before birth, won't that affect how we all think and feel about disabled people after birth? And the pre-natal tests are seeking to find not only Down's Syndrome and neural tube defects but many other genetic and chromosomal disorders.

Are we not really sending this message to born disabled people: you are inferior, you should never have been born. You cost the rest of us money in extra medical care, extra educational tuition, extra everything.

The message to the parents of disabled babies is: you should have had the baby aborted, and instead of being praised for their love and courage they will be criticised, at first covertly and later openly, for their 'selfishness', and not given the support and practical help they need.

Everyone has the right to life

A truly civilised society protects everyone, even those who are not productive and active members. We no longer punish mentally ill people. We pride ourselves on the often amazing advances made in coping with physical and mental disability. So why do we go to such lengths to seek out and kill disabled people before birth? We will not eliminate disability in this way. Most disability is caused *after birth* by disease, accident or the process of growing old.

It's bad for all of us

Disabled people are precious. They have much to contribute. They often bear witness to values which today's world overlooks and can bring out the best in others. They can give and receive much love and joy.

We are all disabled, morally, mentally or physically, to some extent. The 'able-bodied' do well to remember that.

To destroy a child because he or she is not 'perfect' is especially unjust and elitist. Of course it is not always easy to cope. But eugenic abortion re-creates and legitimises primitive phobias and prejudices about mental and physical illness, just when society

seemed to be making real progress in outgrowing them. The policy of 'search and destroy the disabled before birth' is contrary to the tradition of good medicine. It takes away the incentive to find cures. Good medicine consists in trying to conquer diseases, not in killing those who suffer from them.

So much has been achieved in overcoming disabilities. Why jeopardise future progress?

LIFE supports all gene therapy and pre-natal treatment that is designed to help mother and baby, and also post-natal treatment that will either cure or improve disabling conditions.

We also support all statutory and voluntary efforts to give practical and emotional help to parents and children affected by disability.

LIFE cares

LIFE gives skilled counselling to any woman or couple who have been told their unborn child may be disabled. We offer support during pregnancy and after birth. We urge anyone facing this dilemma to contact LIFE.

Helping parents who discover that their baby is abnormal

SATFA (Support Around Termination For Abnormality) is the only national charity offering non-directive, specialised support to parents who discover that their unborn baby is abnormal.

SATFA

- offers support to parents making a decision about antenatal testing, and throughout the antenatal testing process.
- provides support and information to parents who are told that their unborn baby has an abnormality.

- offers ongoing support to those parents who make the decision to end the pregnancy.
- provides a 24 hour helpline: 0171 631 0285.
- refers parents who decide to continue with the pregnancy to appropriate support organisations.

SATFA also:

- co-ordinates a befriending service which offers individual support.
- runs a network of local groups.
- produces a regular newsletter for members.

- distributes a range of highly regarded literature for parents, families and professionals.
- represents the views of parents in parliament, the media, and to decision-makers.
- trains health professionals to meet parent's needs.

Supporting SAFTA

It is only in recent years that terminating a pregnancy because of a fetal abnormality has been recognised as a bereavement, yet it is experienced by more than 2000 families each year.

Popular understanding is that it is only an issue for 'older' pregnant women who may conceive a baby with Down's Syndrome, but every couple has a risk of conceiving a baby with an abnormality, and many SATFA members are under 30. Developments in new technologies and genetics mean that many more parents will face this bereavement: most of them will be healthy young couples with no identifiable risk factors.

More than 1,500 families rely on SATFA for continued support and, together with over 500 specialist health professionals, they receive regu-lar information. Contacts with the SATFA office are currently around 7,000 a year, many of whom use our services on an occasional basis.

Membership of SATFA is open to anybody who supports our aims, although we are parent-centred. We do not charge for membership, but rely entirely on voluntary donations and the sale of materials to fund our work. Securing funding for such a sensitive area of work is always diffi-cult, and donations are therefore very welcome.

A case study

We both wanted children and after trying for only a short time, we were overjoyed when the pregnancy test showed a positive result. I remember touching and talking to my 'bump' even at the start. I had no morning sickness or anything to complain about and even now, with everything we've been through, I don't think we've moaned once. We told every-one the good news and they were all overjoyed for us. My husband serves in the British Army and we live in Germany, so I found it very hard living so far away from family and friends, but with a baby on the way, I put that all behind me and looked excitedly into the future as a family.

As a routine, my midwife explained that they gave all expec-tant mothers a blood test to check Alphafeta protein levels from the babies. Thinking nothing of it, I agreed to have a test done; I was a healthy 21 year old, my husband was a Physical Training Instructor – we had nothing to worry about. We were on Christmas leave in the UK so I

Photo: Brenda Prince / Format

We will never forget our dear son; what we did was right for us

went to my Mum's GP to have the blood taken.

It was Christmas Eve 1993; when the phone rang and the doctor told us that the blood results showed that the baby might have Downs Syn-drome; our lives were shattered. We were sent to the local hospital for a scan; things had somehow along the line got mixed up and the scanning person was told to look for spina bifida in the baby. She spent ages scanning the baby's spine and said everything looked alright and we weren't to worry. I think we took it to heart and thought everything was alright until we saw the GP again who explained the 'mishap', and we were advised to have an amnio-centisis; we did.

I remember being at work when the phone call came through; I spoke to a nurse on the phone; she told me that the results had got mixed up with another parent's. The sex chromosome pots had not been labelled; one was a boy, one was a girl, the boy had Down's – whoever had the male child had a very hard decision to make. I was put on a plane to the UK and was expected at a hospital for a scan to detect our baby's sex; I knew he was a boy.

My husband was away at the time, so I arranged to meet my parents at the hospital. I had the scan; my mum held my hand. It was a boy; I was devastated. My world just fell apart. I was eventually reunited with

my husband and we had to make the biggest decision of our lives.

I was 21, my husband 27; were we old enough to decide to end our baby's life, did we have the right to choose? I was 23 weeks pregnant. We sat and talked all night; we decided to terminate. We were put on another plane back to Germany and I was admitted to the nearest Army hospital. I was to be induced the following morning; our son kept kicking inside me – I prayed for him to stop. I was induced at 10 am; 15 hours later our son came into the world. I was sat on the commode; neither of us could bring ourselves to look at him; we never saw him. I deeply regret that now; we both do; we never said goodbye to him. We had him blessed and had already chosen a name for him. We've since seen his pictures and prints which helped a little. We've also had genetic tests done which show our case was a 'one-off'.

The guilt and the grief is very hard to live and cope with. We will never forget our dear son; what we did was right for us. It would have been harder to watch him live. Even though it was only three months ago, we have started to rebuild our lives but life will never be the same again; there's still one question that will never be answered – Why? Why us? I know we're not alone. God Bless you Elliott.
© SATFA
1994

Face up to the euthanasia debate

An alarming perception is gaining currency that Britain's 'cradle to grave' welfare state is becoming unaffordable, even undesirable. Like other Western nations, we are growing greyer, with ever more people living into their eighties, nineties and beyond. Demographers predict that by the middle of the next century there will not be enough people of working age to provide for the rest of the population, while caring for the elderly forces up the nation's health and social security bills.

At the same time, the seeds of euthanasia are gradually being sprinkled into our collective subconscious. Last month, the state of Oregon became the first place to make it legal. The decision followed the huge publishing success across America of *Final Exit*, the best-selling DIY guide to euthanasia. Pressure will grow for other US states to follow suit. In Holland, euthanasia remains a criminal act, but there are no prosecutions if repeated requests are verified by two doctors. A Dutch film showing a terminally ill man being injected with a sedative, and then a lethal dose, is soon to be shown on BBC television.

Voluntary euthanasia in Britain is an open secret in the Health Service. Each year, evidence mounts that doctors, nurses and relatives, often for the very best of motives, are helping patients to die with dignity rather than have their lives prolonged by medical technology for no clear purpose. Nigel Cox, a consultant rheumatologist from Winchester, was convicted of attempted murder and given a 12 month suspended sentence two years ago after giving a terminally ill elderly woman a lethal injection of potassium chloride. He was not struck off by the General Medical Council. Many doctors said privately that Dr Cox's only error was his choice of drug, a poison with no painkilling properties. If he had used an alternative such as morphine, he could have avoided prosecution by arguing that his intention was to relieve pain – even though the result was the patient's death.

Voluntary euthanasia in Britain is an open secret in the Health Service

Yesterday, we reported that Crown prosecutors decided against charging a man with killing his terminally ill wife, because it did not think a prosecution was in the public interest.

Ending pain is only one reason among many for helping to end life. Sometimes the motives for hastening death seem to have more to do with saving scarce NHS resources than altruism. Last September, *The Observer* reported warnings from Dr Gillian Craig a consultant geriatrician, that euthanasia was creeping into British hospices and hospitals by the back door with no proper debate. The practice was 'medically, ethically and legally dangerous', she said.

So what does the public think? Two surveys published last week provide some insights. The pensioners' magazine, *Yours*, asked its 2,500 readers, whose average age is 69, for their views. Nine out of 10 thought that doctors should be allowed to end the lives of terminally ill people and wanted the law changed; eight out of 10 had told someone they preferred to die rather than suffer in pain. More than half said that they would help a friend, relative or spouse to die in such circumstances.

The second survey, in *The Guardian*, showed that loss of independence is likely to be a much more significant catalyst than pain. The researchers spoke to 3,700

RIP
BORN WITH DIGNITY
DIED WITH DIGNITY
RIP

KenPyne

relatives and friends of people who had just died. Some 28 per cent of respondents and 24 per cent of the deceased expressed the view that an earlier death would have been preferable. More than one third of those over 85 had told others that they wish they had died earlier, compared with only one fifth of those under that age.

This debate does not simply concern the elderly and those who care for them. Tony Bland, who went into a persistent vegetative state as a result of his injuries in the Hillsborough disaster, was only 22 when his life support system was switched off after a High Court ruling allowing doctors to do so. Up to 1,500 people of all ages are still suffering a 'living death' in a persistent vegetative state.

> *The issue is too sensitive and the ethical questions too profound to come to a simple conclusion*

It costs millions to keep them alive, and they may live for 30 years or more.

Increasingly, the fine line between euthanasia and lawfully hastening death is being drawn by the courts. But it is far too important an issue to be left to the judges. Such life and death issues must be a matter of national debate.

Rationing of health care in an ageing society is a reality. None of us knows any longer whether we can rely on the State to take care of us through a long-term illness or disability. This shocking truth, as it sinks in, will stoke up the euthanasia debate still further: most of us are not accustomed to dwelling on our own deaths.

The issue is too sensitive and the ethical questions too profound to come to a simple conclusion. But events are forcing some kind of reform. The Government should appoint a Royal Commission now to ensure that such a sensitive debate is both well informed and conducted in a dignified manner.

© The Observer
December, 1994

Euthanasia: the dilemma of the decade

Euthanasia has become the moral dilemma of the decade.

The facts – for the West, at least – are these: thanks to advances in medical technology, people suffering from chronic illness and disability are living longer and in less (though not necessarily without) pain. At the same time, most of us can now expect to live well past our three score years and ten. A long, frail old age is now routine.

These developments have raised troubling questions. Do we have a duty to preserve the quantity of human life when we may not have the social and economic resources to improve its quality? Does everyone – including those too frail to commit suicide – have the right to end his or her own life? What, for doctors, is the difference between turning off a life-support machine and administering a fatal injection?

The answers have polarised doctors, philosophers, chronically ill people and their families.

In the pro-euthanasia camp are those who argue that there is a right to die. Their members include 2,500 readers of Yours magazine (average age 69), of whom 92 per cent (according to a new survey) support voluntary euthanasia.

> *What, for doctors, is the difference between turning off a life-support machine and administering a fatal injection?*

The BBC has just bought a Dutch film that records the life and death of a chronically ill man who had requested euthanasia. Such views are being heeded. Only this week, the Crown Prosecution Service decided to drop its case against a man who allegedly killed his terminally ill wife to ease her suffering. Meanwhile, in the American state of Oregon, a Death With Dignity Act has just been passed, making it legal for doctors to prescribe a lethal dose of drugs.

The anti-euthanasia camp – though lacking flamboyant figureheads such as Dr Jack Kevorkian, the former pathologist who has been driving a 'suicide machine' around America since June 1990 – is equally impassioned. Euthanasia is the first step towards eugenics, runs the argument. It is not the pain of illness and old age, but its social and economic stigma that is unbearable; a humane society should seek to alleviate both. And nothing can safeguard against misdiagnosis, against pressure from family members. The evidence is powerful: a new survey of 3,696 people in England during 1990 whose friends and relatives had recently died found that fear of becoming dependent was a greater factor than pain among those who supported euthanasia.

© The Independent
December, 1994

Euthanasia: the big debate

Hospice physician, Dr Anthony Smith, explores the controversy

The case for . . .

Sometimes, to some people, death seems preferable to life.

We think of someone who requests termination of life because of terminal illness, incurable disability, pain, suffering and hopelessness.

Surely, they say, to assist such a person to commit suicide, or to help him die when he cannot bring it about for himself, is simply an extension of suicide and ought to be acceptable in a caring society where suicide has been decriminalised.

A powerful case is made for euthanasia by kind and well intentioned people who cite the suffering and distress undergone by some people with terminal illness.

They speak, too, of relatives watching their loved ones die, in cases where the dying person asks, sometimes repeatedly for release from this process of dying.

'You would not treat a dog like this,' they say.

In other cases the relatives claim that the sufferer would commit suicide if he possibly could but does not now have the physical ability to do so, so that euthanasia is surely just enabling him to do what he wishes.

In other circumstances, voluntary euthanasia seems to make economic sense, where otherwise resources are unavailingly expended, for no possible economic value, on behalf of people who have no hope of recovery.

Sometimes, indeed, it is argued that this is a final self-sacrifice that the aged, infirm or terminally ill wish to make on behalf of others.

The case against . . .

Many specialists in palliative care show by reference to patients in hospice care that it should not be necessary for people to suffer unrelieved symptoms in their terminal illness.

And that the answer to requests for euthanasia is that pain, sickness and other distressing symptoms can be effectively relieved these days.

Time and again, patients admitted to a hospice stop asking for euthanasia as good care and control of symptoms make their last days or weeks (or months) worthwhile.

Euthanasia would diminish a person's self-worth. The request for termination of life often springs from a feeling that life is not worth living.

But to respond with euthanasia is to agree that the person's life is worthless. Everyone is inherently worth more than a dog or a cow (or, even, many sparrows!) and his or her very life is worthy of respect.

Here, of course, we are dealing with requests for someone to kill someone else.

For whatever motive it may be done, all religions and civilisations have regarded this as morally wrong.

Exceptions, of course, occur in warfare and (in many societies, though not ours) judicially in judgement on heinous crimes.

But euthanasia is direct and intended killing as a consequence not of crimes committed but of weakness and suffering.

To expect the medical (or nursing), professions to undertake this action would seem an improper extension of their role as carers whose concern was to cure or alleviate suffering.

To expect this to happen in hospitals, hospices or nursing homes is to change the nature of these caring institutions into places of fear.

One of the sadnesses of the recent Dutch experience has been that, whereas a large proportion of younger people have welcomed it, 64 per cent of elderly people in residential homes live in fear that they will be a candidate.

© Chronicle & Echo
February, 1995

The case for legalisation

From the Voluntary Euthanasia Society – EXIT

Set up in 1935, the VES aims to make it legal for a competent adult, who is suffering unbearably from an incurable illness, to receive medical help to die at their own considered and persistent request. Safeguards include: a second medical opinion; psychiatric assessment; wide consultation; advance written request.

A 1994 survey, published in the *British Medical Journal*, showed that over ten per cent of doctors already help patients to die, despite the risk of prosecution. Few doctors have been prosecuted (Dr Nigel Cox, who was reported by a nurse, was an exception), and they have always been treated with great sympathy.

Nearly half of all doctors would be willing to give active help in dying if it were legal, the BMJ survey shows.

Seventy-nine per cent of British people think this should be a legal choice at the end of life, according to a 1993 National Opinion Poll.

Medical advances have actually increased the need for help in dying. Early treatment for killer diseases can keep patients alive for years, but may mean a more painful death in the end. More and more people are living longer but dying of drawn-out degenerative diseases.

Not everyone dies well. About five per cent of terminal pain is uncontrollable, even in hospices. Many other distressing symptoms cannot be relieved. The founder of the hospice movement has written that hospice care can be unavailing.

At the moment, doctors can legally practise 'passive' euthanasia – withholding or withdrawing treatment, or providing pain relief in such high doses that death is hastened. This has exactly the same moral and practical result as actively giving a lethal injection on request.

When the alternatives are death

The Voluntary Euthanasia Society (VES)

with dignity and peace, or death accompanied by prolonged pain and distress, common sense as well as compassion supports the demand that the choice should belong to the individual.

A few miles away across the North Sea, the Dutch have had this choice available to them for many years. Dutch people and Parliament are satisfied with their system.

Some common objections and their rebuttals

Religious objections – only God can give and take away life

Most opposition to the decriminalisation of voluntary euthanasia arises from religious groups, but they do not speak for all religious viewpoints. There are many deeply religious advocates of VE, including VES vice-president Lord Soper. In the Netherlands, Catholic or Dutch Reformed clergymen may be present at VE deaths. In any case, religious arguments cannot apply to anyone who does not share that belief.

A 'slippery slope' – voluntary will soon lead to involuntary

This argument has been used against every social reform, but there is no evidence for it at all. Voluntary

euthanasia as an individual choice is entirely distinct from murdering people who are judged (by others) to have no worth. The VES would NOT support legislation for involuntary euthanasia. Skiers will be vividly aware that being on a slippery slope does not mean going downwards out of control.

Fear of abuse – the impossibility of framing watertight laws

No one knows how much abuse there is because active euthanasia is practised outside the law. If it were brought into the open and strictly controlled, there would be less chance of abuse. At present, doctors allow patients to die, for example by withholding treatment, or not resuscitating. But no one suggests they do so because they 'want the bed free', or out of conspiracy with greedy relatives!

Hospices – palliative care means VE is not necessary

Although palliative care experts do a wonderful job for many people, a tragic few cannot be kept comfortable even in hospices. Others would not want that slow way of dying.

A right to die could become a duty to die

The many people involved in a voluntary euthanasia decision would be likely to judge accurately the sincerity of a patient's wishes. If anything, relatives usually 'bully' the patient to struggle on.

Miracle cures and wrong diagnosis

A patient in hope of a miracle cure would not ask for euthanasia. A doctor who thought one imminent would not do it. A second opinion on the patient's condition will be sought.

Human value or the scrap-heap?

From ALERT which campaigns against the legalisation of euthanasia

By Susan Glyn

The majority of people who support the idea of 'voluntary euthanasia' do so because they are thinking in terms of putting a dying patient out of intolerable pain. In fact, the British Euthanasia Society was founded with just that object. But if we wish to understand the Euthanasia movement as a whole and where it could lead, we must study its history in many countries and the point of view that lies behind it. The phrase 'Mercy Killing' has only recently been adopted in the international campaign for legalised euthanasia The word 'voluntary' is also very much an afterthought. In origin, it was a campaign to 'improve' the human race by eliminating its weaker members.

This was based on the post-Darwinian theory that it was the duty of the strong, not to help the weak, as religion teaches, but to destroy them, in the belief that this would assist human progress. This was known as Social Darwinism. Although the elementary biology on which it was based has long been out-dated in science, the theory still has active supporters, notably among sociologists and political figures in Britain and the United States. The trend of their thought can be seen in examples such as the university debate not long ago in New York, at which one speaker pointed out that the falling birthrate would produce an ageing population; the other speaker replied 'Euthanasia for the over-sixties is going to fix that', and the audience applauded loudly. In a public lecture in Arizona, a scientist recently said 'Social shaping through genetic engineering and euthanasia is no longer theoretical.' This was accepted as common knowledge. It has also been publicly admitted in a population scare pamphlet that the effect on population density of the elimination of all pensioners has been worked out, in a study of the subject. (Happily, the study showed that the removal of all the over-sixties would do little to solve demographic problems.)

Those who are looking to euthanasia to clear overcrowded hospitals or to solve economic problems must be thinking in very much wider terms than hastening the deaths of terminal patients. They must have in mind the aged, the chronically infirm and the mentally ill.

The answer to pain

The agitation to legalise euthanasia has to be seen against this background, even when its ostensible object is to prevent suffering. The stepping-up of propaganda about this to an almost hysterical pitch recently does not correspond to any sudden increase in the number of people dying in pain. On the contrary, the hospice movement, pioneering better care and the more systematic use of improved drugs has greatly reduced the problem. If enough support is given to extending this work, dying need not be associated with the word 'agony' any more. As a district nurse said, in a human rights television programme, hospice care 'makes euthanasia an outdated concept'. Although this is now well known in medical circles, the pressure to change the law, or to ignore it, continues to increase in many countries, almost as if the agitators (or some of them) realise that the justification for doing so is rapidly being removed, and feel that they must rush through their legislation before the public finds this out.

● The above is an extract from *Human Value or the Scrap-heap*, available from Alert. See page 39 for address details.

The need for voluntary euthanasia

Introduction

It is natural to hope that when the time comes we shall die peacefully, with dignity and without prolonged suffering. Those who do so will be fortunate, for many must still endure a long drawn out and deeply distressing process of degeneration.

There is a strong case, based on common sense and compassion, for granting the wish of incurable patients for a merciful release from prolonged and useless suffering. The late Rev Dr Leslie Weatherhead, the prominent Methodist, said:

'I sincerely believe that those who come after us will wonder why on earth we kept a human being alive against his own will, when all the dignity, beauty and meaning of life had vanished; when any gain to anyone was clearly impossible, and when we should have been punished by the State if we had kept an animal alive in similar physical conditions.'

Misunderstandings and misrepresentations

One would expect general approval of such a humane and compassionate aim. There is, indeed, ample evidence of rapidly growing support in this country and overseas. But as the campaign to legalise voluntary euthanasia gathers support and momentum, so does the campaign of our opponents.

The purpose of this article is to state the case for voluntary euthanasia. Before doing this, however, we need to dispose of three of the most common misunderstandings and misrepresentations.

- The VES does not advocate 'getting rid of the old, the infirm and the unwanted'.

  On the contrary, the Society believes that the care of the old, the sick and the dying should be a paramount obligation upon any humane society.

- The VES does not advocate 'putting down' handicapped babies, or the mentally disabled, or any other vulnerable group. We seek only the legalisation of *voluntary* euthanasia, under strict conditions.

- The VES does not advocate 'suicide on demand', nor is it prepared to act in breach of the existing law. Under no circumstances, therefore, can the Society help anyone to commit suicide, either by giving direct assistance, or by providing personal advice.

Is voluntary euthanasia necessary?

The hospice movement has improved the care of the dying and some of its supporters claim that it has eliminated the need for voluntary euthanasia. While we welcome and admire the work of hospice doctors and nurses, we regard the giving of voluntary euthanasia, when that time comes, as the final act of care and respect for the autonomous patient.

The VES believes that voluntary euthanasia should be just one of a range of options at the end of life. Hospices represent another available option. But at the end, we believe it is a human right to have a choice about the manner of your death.

Even with hospice care, some terminally ill people have to suffer severe and continuous distress. Pain can be reduced by the repeated use of narcotics and sedative drugs, but often at the cost of nausea, constipation, deterioration of the personality, and other side-effects. But sadly, not everyone can be kept free from pain.

Palliative care experts, often hospice doctors, accept that approximately 5% of terminal pain cannot be controlled.

In addition to pain, feelings of nausea, of suffocation or of being desperately ill cannot always be relieved. Cancer patients may have to suffer the mental misery associated with the presence of a foul growth, obstruction of the bowels, or incontinence, and the utter frustration that makes each day and night a death in life. Diseases of the nervous system all too often lead to crippling paralysis or inability to walk, to severe headaches, to blindness and to the misery of incontinence and bedsores. Bronchitis, with its interminable cough and progressive shortness of breath, can have its special terrors which medical treatment can do little to abate in the late stages.

Likewise, patients with a stroke may be conscious but helpless. Their misery is frequently overlooked.

It is accepted by hospices that any claims that patients can always avoid distressing symptoms are exaggerated.

The VES receives a great many letters telling of prolonged pain and considerable distress endured by dying friends and relatives. These stress the continuing reality of the problem, despite all recent medical advances.

When the alternatives are death with dignity and peace, or death accompanied by prolonged pain and distress, common sense as well as compassion support our demand that the choice should belong to individuals. As the law now stands, they have no choice: their wishes count for nothing.

The Netherlands is the only country in the world where voluntary euthanasia is practised by doctors without fear of prosecution if they follow strict guidelines. Only Dutch citizens will be considered, and so they are the only people to have a full choice about the manner of their death. Some 2,300 Dutch people a year receive medical help to die at their own considered request.

The 1961 Suicide Act

Since the Suicide Act, which passed without opposition in 1961, it is no longer a criminal act to commit suicide or attempt to do so.

This Act therefore recognised the right of individuals to decide when their own life was unbearable, and was an important development. But it still leaves both doctor and patient in a difficult and unsatisfactory position, since the Act says that 'a person who aids, abets, counsels or procures the suicide of another, or an attempt by another to commit suicide, shall be liable on conviction on indictment to imprisonment for a term not exceeding fourteen years'.

Terminal patients suffering extreme distress seldom have the knowledge, the means or the capacity to end their own lives, particularly if they are in hospital. They need the help of a doctor to obtain release from suffering. But a doctor who carries out the patient's wishes is risking prosecution.

The campaign for change

It was public concern about making the act of dying more gentle that led in 1935 to the founding of this Society under the presidency of the most progressive English surgeon of that time, the late Lord Moynihan. In 1936, in the House of Lords, a Bill was promoted which sought to permit voluntary euthanasia in certain circumstances and with certain safeguards. Lord Dawson of Penn, the royal physician, argued eloquently that legalisation was unnecessary since 'good' doctors already helped their patients to die if the need arose. As we know now, he spoke from impressive practical experience, having just ended the life of King George V.

The Bill was rejected on the Second Reading, but the discussion was sympathetic and public disquiet about the problem of being helped to die peacefully continued to grow.

There have been several similarly unsuccessful attempts to introduce Bills in the House of Lords.

In 1988 the VES began a Parliamentary campaign, and in 1991 an independent All Party Parliamentary Voluntary Euthanasia

Photo: Voluntary Euthanasia Society

Sir Dirk Bogarde, vice-president of the Voluntary Euthanasia Society

Group was formed with members from both Houses of Parliament and from all the major political parties. The primary activity of the group was to consider a Bill to confirm the legal status of advance directives for health care.

The Bill received its first reading in the House of Lords in March 1993 and was then presented as evidence to a House of Lords Select Committee on Medical Ethics, which is examining all aspects of euthanasia. The Committee, whilst commending the use of advance directives, thought that legislation was unnecessary. However, the government is now awaiting the recommendations of the Law Commission, which is due to report later this year.

Public opinion

In April 1993 a National Opinion Poll found that 79% agreed that 'the law should allow adults to receive medical help to a peaceful death if suffering from an incurable illness that is intolerable to them, provided that they have previously requested such help in writing'. Only 10% disagreed.

Every Christian denomination as well as other religions produced a majority in favour. The highest figure for a religious denomination was the Church of Scotland (85%) with the Church of England/Anglicans at 80%. Roman Catholics showed 73% in favour. 60% of Jewish people were in agreement.

A second question asked the same people whether they had known someone who had suffered within the previous five years from such an illness. 38% said they had, showing that the problem is very real.

The number of people supporting voluntary euthanasia has risen dramatically over the years. In February 1985, 72% agreed that the law should be changed, and in September 1976 the figure was only 69%.

Polls in various States of America and Australia, and also in European countries, also show large majorities in favour of the legalisation of voluntary euthanasia.

● The above is an extract from *The Last Right*, available from the Voluntary Euthanasia Society. See page 39 for address details.

© *Voluntary Euthanasia Society*
January, 1995

The relief of pain

**From The Human Rights Trust which opposes
attempts to decriminalise euthanasia**

The Human Rights Trust does not believe in euthanasia . . . that implies failure of care. Nor do we believe in the artificial prolonging of life by machine, or officious striving to keep alive for a little while those who are obviously dying and who cannot, through good treatment, be restored to health. Painful treatment which cannot succeed is, of course, totally different from treatment for such conditions as, for example, a heart attack, or a stroke, which is reversible. That kind of treatment is to be welcomed.

But, although we do not believe in the deliberate taking of life for any reason, neither do we believe that the terminally ill should be allowed to suffer. For just as pain can be relieved during and after surgical operations, and in chronic conditions such as arthritis or migraine, so, with care and attention, it can be relieved in distressing terminal illness.

If a patient does not receive relief from his pain it is usually for one or more of three reasons:

1 He is not receiving the most suitable drug or combination of drugs.
2 He is not receiving a sufficiently strong dose.
3 The drug(s) is/are not being given often enough.

The third point is extremely important, for all too often an effective drug is given in an adequate dosage but its effect is allowed to wear off before the next dose is given. Because this is so, the patient knows that his pain will return. This engenders fear. He tends to watch the clock, waiting for pain. And this fear can actually make pain worse, as his resistance is lowered through unnecessary apprehension.

There are many drugs that can be given to relieve pain. Some are far stronger than others. They have a different length of effectiveness. Some, for instance, wear off very quickly – within two to three hours (for example pethidine or Fortral). Others last between six and eight hours. Most come somewhere in between, with relief lasting for about four full hours before the effect starts to wear off. This means that if these drugs are given six hourly, as is very often the case, the final two hours before the next dose is a time of steadily increasing pain. If, on the other hand, the drug is given four-hourly by the clock, before the pain returns, and therefore before the patient feels the need for a repeat, relief is maintained continuously.

This is the basis of the pain-relief regime used in hospices. It can be used just as effectively by and for patients at home. Not all, by any means, need the very strong drugs. But even with the milder analgesics, this four-hourly by-the-clock regime is the best way to keep pain at bay, alleviate fear of pain, and so make life worth living, no matter how short the time that remains.

Discomforts other than pain can make life miserable for the terminally ill or chronically sick person in need of continuing drug therapy. Nausea, constipation or diarrhoea, lack of appetite, confusion, insomnia and depression can all add to distress. As with pain, none of these are inevitable. For there are effective drugs and nursing measures which can cope adequately to bring relief.

Just knowing that such relief is available can do a lot to change the mood of the sick person. Some who ask for so-called 'mercy killing' are, in fact, clinically depressed. With their pain and depression relieved, a patient's whole attitude may change for the better. All the necessary drugs can be prescribed by the family doctor if the patient is at home.

Issued by Human Rights
March, 1995

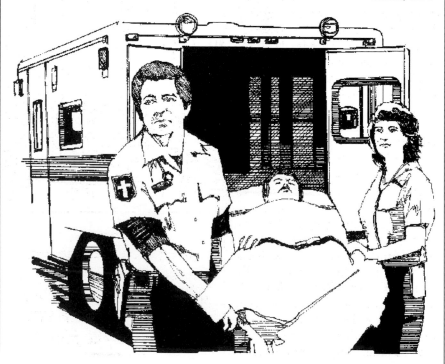

Dutch watch euthanasia on television

...at
...er
...ry
...nt
...on
...t.
...is
...e
...-
...t
...f.

sclerosis. When the documentary begins he is confined to a wheelchair, has a paralysed shoulder, and cannot write or talk properly.

Van Wendel communicates with his general practitioner, and the camera, by pointing to letters on an alphabet board, which his wife speaks. He has explained to his general practitioner and hospital consultant that he does not want to enter hospital or be put on a respirator. He has asked for euthanasia and hopes to survive until his birthday some months away. He writes in his diary, 'The possibility of euthanasia has been a consoling thought all these months. It has kept me going.'

Dr Wilfred van Oijen, his general practitioner, talks to the camera, saying that there is no choice and no remedy for his patient and that his role as a doctor is to prevent suffering. Dr van Oijen is filmed talking to his patient, consoling his wife, and consulting with a neurologist.

The documentary ends on Mr van Wendel's birthday. He drinks his last glass of port from a straw and says, 'Let's not postpone this any more,' before driving his motorised wheelchair into his bedroom, where his wife helps him on to his deathbed. The camera then follows as Dr van Oijen prepares and gives two injections; the first sends Mr van Wendel to sleep and the second kills him, as the doctor consoles his wife. Mr Schenk explained that originally the documentary was to end at the bedroom door, but the trust that was built up with the couple meant that the camera team was 'invited to stay.' IKON claims that after the documentary 20 telephone counselling lines received more than 200 calls, of which 90% praised the film – Tony Sheldon, freelance journalist, Utrecht

© BMJ volume 309 – October, 1994

...ed by a team of doctors, searching for an appropriate case and awaiting permission to film. This was finally given by Cees van Wendel de Joode, a restaurant owner, and his wife, Anthionette. He suffered from the rapidly debilitating neurological disorder amyotrophic lateral

---

After the documentary 20 telephone counselling lines received more than 200 calls, of which 90% praised the film

---

I sat holding his hand until he was dead

The spouse

Ruth is a 70 year old former teacher. Five years ago she helped her husband, an academic, to die.

My husband was a social anthropologist. He retired in 1983, but continued to be a very active man. Then, seven years into his retirement, he was found to be suffering from multiple sclerosis. It is unusual to develop the condition over the age of 60, and he was 69. He refused to give in to it, sleeping upstairs although he often had to drag his feet over every step.

But while he fought physically, psychologically he became angry, bitter and frightened. Then a serious infection robbed him completely of his mobility. He could not even roll over in bed and became incontinent. The doctors did all they could but it was clear that he would never recover the use of his body.

Then he began to have trouble with his eyes. It was bad enough being unable to walk over and take a book from the shelf; to face the prospect of being unable to read it was the final straw. If it had been a question of dying in six months' time, he said he might have been able to cope, but he knew he might go on living for years.

The situation was intolerable for him and he attempted to commit suicide by suffocation with a plastic bag. But because of his condition, this was too difficult for him.

It was then that I realised I could not allow someone with whom I had lived for 40 years, whom I loved, to set off on such a journey alone. I told him if he was absolutely sure he wanted to end his life, then I would be there to ensure it happened. He said: 'Please don't feel you have to, but that would be wonderful.'

> **I told him if he was absolutely sure he wanted to end his life, then I would be there to ensure it happened**

In the following days, the years seemed to fall away from his face and his bitterness and anger disappeared. There had been a good deal of strain in our marriage because of his illness, but in those last days we were very much together. I had to make sure there was no one in the house and he told me not to call for help too soon afterwards because the emergency services might be able to resuscitate him.

I found in myself a residue of strength which I suppose we all have. I wasn't crying – this was too important for that. I sat holding his hand until he was dead. I then sat with him through the night. It was a time of thought and a great many memories. I was glad he wasn't going to suffer anymore, that he had escaped. I told the police I had come downstairs in the morning and found him dead.

We have three children and I told them, and my husband's close friends and family, exactly what had happened. I didn't want them thinking that he had committed suicide in a state of despair. They knew the option he had taken was right for him. He had been a member of the Voluntary Euthanasia Society and firmly believed that everyone should be able to choose when to die.

The memory of his courage at the end of his life is far from ghastly. Not a day goes by without me thinking of him.

© The Independent
December, 1994

His pain was too much for him to bear

The doctor

Dr Stephen Henderson Smith worked for the Missionary Society in China during the Second World War and as a doctor in the Belgian Congo before returning to Britain in 1956 to become a GP in Huddersfield. He retired in 1992.

A doctor's job is to relieve suffering and that is something which can never be done by procrastination. Why should one allow nature to take its long and painful course when you have the means to help people immediately? One of my first patients, an elderly man, had pneumonia which, in 1942 when the supply of antibiotics was inadequate and penicillin wasn't available, was considered a terminal illness. He begged me to help him die. His pain was too much for him to bear. I struggled for days with my conscience and eventually, I gave him a dose of morphine that was just over the usual limit. I remember thinking if death occurs, so be it. I wanted to release him.

Ten years ago a man I had never seen before came into my surgery just as I was about to leave and asked to be seen as a private patient. He was in his late seventies and had bronchitis and emphysema. Every breath he took was agony. He told me that he wanted to end his life. I said that I couldn't risk the legal complications, but he was so desirous of a way out of his pain and suffering that he begged me, 'If you can't do it, at least tell me how many of my tablets I should take to be sure of death.' I wrote '30' on a piece of paper.

The following week I read in the local paper that he had died. For some time I felt very nervous that I would be arrested. People knew my views on euthanasia A doctor who raises his head above the parapet is asking for trouble.

The medical establishment's attitude to ending life is the same as a century ago. Radical change is needed. There should of course be adequate legal safeguards, and I would also like to see a religious service with hymns and the person in question surrounded by loved ones before being taken into a side room for a lethal injection. Suicide is a lonely and miserable end to someone's life. Why should an individual feel forced to take that option?

I live alone now and my purpose for living is my children and grandchildren.

I dread them having to put me in a nursing home and draining all their resources while I wait for a telegram from the Queen. What kind of a life would that be for them? And what kind of an end would that be for me? Lonely and miserable.

© The Independent

The Netherlands guidelines

On allowing and helping to die

- There must be a physical or mental suffering which the sufferer finds unbearable.
- The suffering and the desire to die must be lasting (i.e. not temporary).
- The decision, to die must be the voluntary decision of an informed patient.
- The patient must have a correct and clear understanding of his or her condition and its prognosis. He or she must be capable of weighing the available options and must have done so.
- The time and manner of death must not cause unavoidable misery to others (i.e. if possible the next of kin should be informed and the patient should put their affairs in reasonable order).
- There must be no other solution that is acceptable to the patient.
- The decision to give aid in dying must not be a one-person decision. Consulting another professional is obligatory.
- A medical doctor must be involved in the decision and in prescribing the correct drugs.
- The decision process and the actual aid must be done with the utmost care.
- The person receiving aid in dying need not be terminally ill, e.g. they could be paraplegic.

In 1984 the Netherlands Medical Association accepted these ethical standards as guidelines for the practice of voluntary euthanasia. In 1990 the Dutch Solicitor General announced a reporting procedure. Doctors report cases of voluntary euthanasia to the coroner, and if the guidelines have been strictly adhered to, doctors are not prosecuted. In 1993 the Dutch Parliament voted to legalise this reporting procedure.

© The Voluntary Euthanasia Society
January, 1995

Current legislation

From the Voluntary Euthanasia Society – EXIT

There is no legislation dealing directly with 'mercy killing' or voluntary euthanasia. The law which applies is that which forbids murder. This carries a mandatory sentence of life imprisonment, however in many cases of 'mercy killing', the charge has been reduced to manslaughter under Section.2 (1) and (3) of the Homicide Act:

Homicide Act 1957

Diminished responsibility

Section.2 (1). 'Where a person kills or is party to the killing of another, he shall not be convicted of murder if he was suffering from such abnormality of mind . . . as substantially to impair his mental responsibility for his acts and omissions in doing or being party to the killing.'

Section.2 (3). 'A person who but for this section would be liable, whether as principal or as accessory, to be convicted of murder shall be liable instead to be convicted of manslaughter.'

Suicide pacts

Section.4 (1) 'It shall be manslaughter and shall not be murder for a person acting in pursuance of a suicide pact between him and another to kill the other or to be a party to the other being killed by a third party.'

Note 1. Mercy killing

In 1976, the Criminal Law Revision Committee suggested that as an alternative to a charge of murder, there should be a new offence which would apply to a person who from compassion kills another person who is or is believed by him to be (1) permanently subject to great bodily pain or suffering or (2) permanently helpless from bodily or mental incapacity or (3) subject to rapid and incurable bodily or mental degeneration. The proposal did not necessarily require the consent of the deceased and a maximum penalty of 2 years imprisonment was proposed. Many other groups and individuals have supported this proposal, but it has not been pursued.

Note 2

The Homicide Act 1957 applies to England and Wales, and (with minor differences) to Scotland.

Suicide Act 1961

Since 1961 in England and Wales suicide has not been a crime, but assisting is. The relevant parts of the law are:

Section.2 (1). 'A person who aids, abets, counsels or procures the suicide of another, or an attempt by another to commit suicide, shall be liable on conviction on indictment to imprisonment for a term not exceeding fourteen years.'

Section.2 (2) 'If on the trial of an indictment for murder or manslaughter it is proved that the accused aided, abetted, counselled or procured the suicide of the person in question, the jury may find him guilty of that offence.'

Notes on the Suicide Act 1961

1 The case of R v McShane (1977) established that an attempt at assistance, even though no suicide takes place, is also punishable under the Act.

2 Prosecutions, which have to authorised by the Director of Public Prosecutions, have been few. The usual penalty has been probation or a suspended sentence, though imprisonment is not unknown. In the McShane case the sentence was imprisonment for two years.

3 In view of Section.2 (1), the legality of the Society's booklet *A Guide to Self-Deliverance* was questioned and became the subject of a civil action brought by the Attorney General in April 1983. The judge then took the view that in some (though not all) circumstances distribution would be punishable under the criminal law.

© The Voluntary Euthanasia Society
January, 1995

Yes, *help me to die*

Two and a half thousand completed survey forms were used used to compile the results on these pages. Thousands more *Yours* readers responded.

Who took part

The average age was 69½, with 44 per cent of people being in the 65 to 74 age bracket. Twenty per cent were aged between 55 and 64, and 26 per cent between 75 and 84 years.

Fifty-four per cent, the largest number of you who responded, said your health was good although 39 per cent would describe their state of health as fair.

Most of the replies – 85 per cent – came from women.

Do you let others know how you feel?

A staggering 80 per cent of you confirmed that you had expressed sentiments such as 'Please don't let me suffer if I am in pain and there is no hope for me.' Yet, when it came to discussing the matter of voluntary euthanasia with your doctor, 87 per cent of you replied no, you hadn't talked to him or her about it.

When asked to respond to the statement 'I want to discuss euthanasia with my family but don't feel I can', 34 per cent agreed with the statement, 51 per cent did not agree and 15 per cent weren't sure.

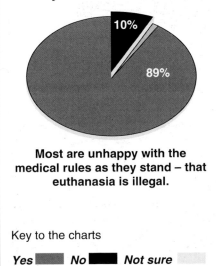

Most are unhappy with the medical rules as they stand – that euthanasia is illegal.

Key to the charts

Yes ▬ **No** ■ **Not sure** ▬

Are you happy with the present situation?

Are you happy with the medical rules as they stand – that euthanasia is illegal?' Eighty-nine per cent of you are definitely unhappy, 10 per cent were content and 1 per cent were not sure.

But, in your opinion, life could be made much better for the terminally ill: 96 per cent felt that more resources should be spent on hospice care and pain relief so that a person's death could be serene and painless.

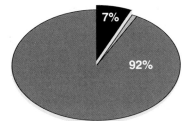

Most believe doctors should be permitted to assist in ending life on request.

Our right or murder?

'No' was the overwhelming response to the question 'Do you believe euthanasia is murder?' Ninety-two per cent of you gave the thumbs down to that suggestion. To the statement 'I believe life is a gift of God and should not be taken away,' 75 per cent said no, 13 per cent agreed and 12 per cent weren't sure.

Again 92 per cent of you believe that doctors should be permitted to assist in ending your life, should you wish them to do so.

Being a burden on your family is felt by many to be a reason for actively persuading someone to help you end your life – 78 per cent agreed with this.

But nearly everyone, 93 per cent, believe that voluntary euthanasia is their own decision. But if you

were incapable of communicating the wish to be helped to die, 90 per cent would want a loved one to make the decision to end your life if you were terminally ill and suffering increasingly.

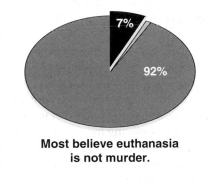

Most believe euthanasia is not murder.

Who decides?

A majority felt that the patient should make the ultimate decision when to let a terminally ill patient die – 56 per cent. Forty-two per cent would like the doctor to make the decision and 9 per cent would like it to be an agreement between the doctor and the patient's relatives.

A large percentage – 89 – did not believe that a doctor who administers a substance to hasten death (where relatives have agreed) was 'playing God' and 89 per cent believe that 'mercy killing' already goes on unofficially.

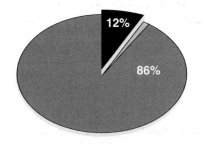

Would you want the power to demand that a dearly beloved person who was terminally ill, and in pain, be 'helped to die'? 'Yes', said most readers in the survey.

Opinion was more spread on the question, 'If voluntary euthanasia were legalised, would it create the possibility for the unscrupulous to end your life without your consent?' 61 per cent said no, 29 per cent said yes and 11 per cent weren't sure.

Helping loved ones

When asked if you would want the power to demand that a dearly beloved person who was terminally ill and in increasing pain be 'helped to die' 86 per cent of you said yes.

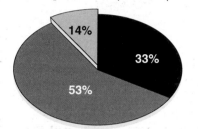

Most would assist a friend, relative or spouse to end their life.

The reaction was not so positive to the statement 'I would assist a friend, relative or spouse to end their life' 53 per cent said yes, 33 per cent replied no and the 'not sure' response was larger for this than any other section.

Making your own wishes known

The Voluntary Euthanasia Society provide an Advance Directive (or Living Will) which is lodged with

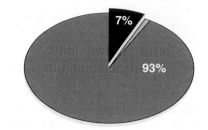

When we asked: 'Do you think that you would be happier if the dread of a lingering and painful death were removed?', most said: 'Yes.'

your doctor and states your wishes. Only 13 per cent of you have made a Living Will. In response to the statement 'Everyone should make a Living Will expressing their views on euthanasia,' 84 per cent agreed.

Making you happier

Finally the response to the question 'Do you think you would be happier if the dread of a lingering and painful death were removed?' Ninety-three per cent of you said yes.

The debate continues

We've asked church leaders, the British Medical Association, the Voluntary Euthanasia Society and other influential figures for their views on the results of the *Yours* survey.

Scots support mercy killing

By Kerry Gill and Anna Smith

Two out of three Scots now back mercy killing, it was revealed yesterday. And more than half believe that euthanasia – helping the old and terminally ill to die – should be made legal.

The survey by the BBC comes just hours after a US court ruling made Oregon the first state in the world to legalise the right to die. 'The US bill and the overwhelming backing of Scots for euthanasia is great news,' said Christopher Docker of the Voluntary Euthanasia Society of Scotland. 'This will give hope to thousands who face a lingering and undignified death.' Clerical assistant Elaine Darling, 28, from Edinburgh, who has breast cancer, agrees.

She said: 'I have told my family, my doctor, and our minister that, if I become so ill there is no hope, I don't want to be kept alive.' Although the US move has been temporarily blocked by another court ruling, it's likely to go ahead. And

that could open the floodgates for many Western countries giving people the right to die by law.

But there are fears about it. The matron of St Andrew's Hospice in Airdrie, Lanarkshire, Sister Catherine, said: 'People have to be able to come to terms with death in its own time. If euthanasia was legalised, there is a danger that people might ask for it when they are at a very low point in their lives.' In Britain, doctors can allow people suffering an irreversible illness to die. And they can increase pain-killing drug doses which can shorten a patient's life. But this is a very thin line to tread. The doctor cannot be seen to be aiding death, only relieving pain.

Spokesmen for the Catholic Church and the Church of Scotland opposed euthanasia. The Catholic spokesman said life was God-given and that nobody had the right to interfere with it.

And the BMA in Scotland said: 'Active euthanasia should remain illegal. More emphasis should be put on increasing knowledge of pain control and care methods.' Scots journalist and TV personality Ludovic Kennedy yesterday welcomed the US move. He said he had supported euthanasia since hearing his own mother say she wanted to die.

And 73 year old Kennedy renewed his attack on the Catholic hierarchy – particularly the Pope – for opposing euthanasia.

He said they were out of step with public thinking.

Kennedy has branded the Pope 'medieval and barbaric' for his stand against mercy killing, citing polls which show 73 per cent of Catholics want the right to decide when to die.

He has called for next year's Lib-Dem conference in Glasgow to debate legalising euthanasia.

Relatives keener on euthanasia than patients

People in Britain are more likely to request euthanasia to avoid being a burden to their relatives than because they are in pain, according to a new study. Clive Seale, a lecturer in the sociology of medicine at Goldsmith's College, London, and Julia Addington-Hall, an epidemiologist from University College London, asked 2192 people who had recently been bereaved about their experiences. They were asked whether the dying person had expressed a wish to die earlier and whether he or she had requested euthanasia.

Relatives were asked whether the person would have benefited from an earlier death. Over a third of the respondents were spouses, nearly half were other relatives, and the remainder were friends, neighbours, or officials such as wardens of sheltered accommodation.

Overall, 28% of respondents said that it would have been better for the person to have died earlier. Spouses were the least likely to think that the person should have died earlier, and this remained true after the person's age and levels of pain and dependency had been controlled for. Children, friends, and officials were more likely to say that an earlier death would have been desirable.

Less than 4% of the people who died had expressed a wish for euthanasia, though nearly a quarter had expressed some desire for an earlier death. The researchers write in the *Journal of Social Science and Medicine*: 'Respondents who were not spouses were more willing to say that an earlier death would have been better even though the person who died had not said they wanted to die sooner.' There were no differences in responses between those people with religious beliefs and those without.

Relative attitudes

The Survey, by researchers Clive Seale and Julia Addington-Hall, questioned 3,696 people in 20 health authorities in England during 1990 about friends and relatives who had recently died. The main findings were:

- 28 per cent of respondents and 24 per cent of the deceased had expressed the view that an earlier death would have been preferable.
- 3.6 per cent of those who died were said to have asked for euthanasia at some point in the last year of their life.
- Fear of becoming dependent was a greater factor than pain among most of those who expressed these wishes. Those dying from cancer, however, were more likely to be motivated by pain.
- 35 per cent of those over 85 said they wished they had died earlier, compared with 20 per cent of those under that age.
- Religious faith, social class and place of residence had little bearing on people's views about euthanasia.
- Husbands and wives were less likely than others to feel it would have been better if the person had died earlier. Conversely, other carers – including friends, relatives, neighbours and officials – were more likely to say an earlier death would have been preferable.
- People who received hospice care were, if anything, more likely to feel it would have been better if they had died earlier.

The first part of the survey appeared in Social Science and Medicine, vol 39, no 5, earlier this year.
© The Guardian, February, 1995

The desire to die sooner was associated with higher levels of dependency and being cared for in a hospice. People dying of cancer who received hospice services were twice as likely as others to have asked for euthanasia at some point during their last year.

'This is the first substantial report to look at the views of people who have been through bereavement,' said Clive Seale. 'Most of the opinion polls suggest a religious element to people's objections to euthanasia. We find that religion makes no difference when people are considering what they want for themselves. Opinion polls can only ask in the abstract – our study finds out what actually happened when these people died. The study shows that there is not a simple relationship between quality of care and the wish to die. It's more complicated than simply providing good care. People in hospices feel more able to talk about death.' Seale said that the study did not support or condemn euthanasia. 'It does provide some evidence for those who oppose euthanasia because they fear that elderly and vulnerable people can be abused. It shows that there are old people being looked after by people who don't have a large emotional investment in their lives continuing and are able to see the positive side of their dying earlier.'

© BMJ Volume 309
October, 1994

'One in four' GPs get pleas for euthanasia

By Chris Mihill
Medical Correspondent

One in four family doctors has had a request from patients to help them die within the past 12 months, and one in ten has been asked several times, a survey published today says.

Over their careers, more than 60 per cent of GPs and half of hospital doctors have been asked by patients to hasten their deaths.

The survey, published in *Doctor* magazine, says that half the GPs wish they could comply with such requests. Overall, 44 per cent felt the law should be changed so that it is similar to that in the Netherlands, where euthanasia, although illegal, is not the subject of criminal charges.

The survey, covering 2,150 GPs and hospital doctors, was self-selected, in that the doctors had to write in to the magazine, but the findings are similar to previous studies. Eight out of ten said they thought passive euthanasia – where treatment is withheld as opposed to giving lethal injections or drugs with active euthanasia – was an accepted part of medical practice. Nearly half, 43 per cent, said they would consider practising euthanasia if it were legal.

Requests by patients or relatives for speedier death were prompted by mental distress in 35 per cent of cases and unbearable pain in 35 per cent, with poor outlook, age, and brain damage cited as other reasons.

There were sharp regional variations, with 68 per cent of doctors in East Anglia having been asked by a patient to hasten death, but only 47 per cent in Ulster.

The British Medical Association yesterday reiterated its long-held position that the law on euthanasia should not be changed, but doctors should be given better training in pain relief and care of the dying.

Stuart Horner, chairman of the BMA's medical ethics committee, said that the doctors who replied to the survey were just half of one per cent of all doctors in the country.

> *Over their careers, more than 60 per cent of GPs and half of hospital doctors have been asked by patients to hasten their deaths*

The Voluntary Euthanasia Society welcomed the survey, especially the finding that nearly half of doctors wanted the law changed. 'The tide is clearly turning. Those who oppose wider choice at the end of life are like King Canute trying to hold back the sea.

'People want the option of voluntary euthanasia, and many doctors are willing to give their patients this merciful release. How long will the law continue to make compassionate doctors into criminals? How long will the law ignore the suffering of ordinary people?'

A survey published in the *British Medical Journal* in May last year by Patricia Tate found that six out of 10 GPs and consultants had been asked by patients to hasten their deaths. Thirty-eight of the 273 doctors who completed an anonymous questionnaire said they had taken active steps to end a patient's life, and half said they would use euthanasia if it were legal.

A study published last year among 3,695 people whose friends or relatives had recently died found that a quarter of the deceased had expressed a wish to die earlier in their final illness, and 28 per cent of the friends or relatives said an earlier death would have been preferable.

© The Guardian
February, 1995

Doctor euthanasia survey

	Would you consider practising euthanasia if it were made legal?		Should the law be changed so it is similar to that in the Netherlands?	
	Yes	No	Yes	No
North	45%	53%	44%	55%
Midlands	46%	52%	45%	52%
East Anglia	48%	48%	49%	47%
London	40%	56%	42%	56%
South East	41%	56%	44%	55%
South West	49%	51%	48%	49%
Wales	48%	52%	48%	52%
Scotland	42%	56%	43%	54%
Ulster	26%	73%	30%	67%
Total	43%	54%	44%	54%

© Doctor, 1994

A flicker of hope

One hospital's progress is adding to the controversy over whether to pull the plug on 'hopeless' coma cases

The decision by doctors to pull the plug on Hillsborough victim Tony Bland led to a stormy debate about the rights and wrongs of 'hopeless' medical cases. Now one hospital is pioneering a programme of coma arousal therapy to give their families new hope.

Mark Newton, 27, suffered brain damage after a diving accident. It took 17 hours, rather than the recommended 45 minutes, to put him in a decompression chamber when he got the bends. But Mark can now talk, touch type, walk with a frame and is currently a student on a business studies course.

Mark, who only narrowly escaped becoming an unwilling organ donor in South Africa, believes that while he was in his 'waking coma,' he could actually hear and understand everything that was going on around him.

'My dad brought me a Walkman and a Van Morrison tape,' recalls Mark; 'The nurses used to come by and say, "Oh, look at him. He's listening to his tape. Are you enjoying

One hospital is poineering a programme of coma arousal therapy to give their families new hope

it, then?" And I'd be saying. "No, it stopped hours ago," but no words came out and they couldn't hear me.

'It was peculiar. I felt very peaceful and didn't realise I couldn't move.

'The doctors don't understand how and why, but they know it's true because I know all sorts of things that happened when I was in a coma and there's no other explanation for that knowledge.

'As I came out, my mother told me a cousin had had a baby. "I know. It was a little girl," I said. "How do you know that?" she asked, amazed. "He told me when he came in to see me," I said. "But you were in a coma then." Some people say it's a miracle.'

Of course, not every case is as hopeful as Mark's. Danny, was

admitted to the Hospital in Putney five months after problems with the oxygen flow to his brain caused by diabetes complications. So far, he has unfortunately made little progress.

The staff at the hospital, however, are not discouraged. 'Quality of life is only something that the individual concerned can assess,' says Dr Keith Andrews, 'I have known a great many people who say that they wouldn't wish to live after a stroke. But then they've had a stroke and changed their minds. They've decided that they really do want to live.

'We've looked at our patients and very few express the view that they wish they had not been saved. We try to find ways to bring the best quality of life to every patient, no matter what their disability.' Mark puts it another way. 'I really don't think that PVS should continue to stand for persistent vegetative state,' he said, 'Instead, it should stand for Putney's very special.'

© *Best Magazine, September, 1994*

INDEX

abortifacient drugs 4, 12
abortion
    as contraception 4
        as murder 4, 6
    back-alley 4, 8
    by country 3
    different methods 13
    global views 1, 2
    health risks 1, 6, 11, 17
    in Britain 5, 9
    myths 17
    rate 9
    statistics 1, 9, 17
Abortion Act 11
abortion clinics 15, 16
adoption 4, 7
    children 4
Alert 25
anti-abortion groups 4, 5, 17

Birth Control Trust 5, 15
British Euthanasia Society 25

Christians for Free Choice 11
consent
    doctors' 11, 17
    parents' 12, 18
    woman's 12
contraception 2, 9, 13

Death on Request 29
Department of Health 12
diminished responsibility 32
disabilities 18, 19, 26

economic factors 9, 17, 22
Education for Choice 11
effects of abortion
    emotional 5, 9, 13
    physical 8, 13
    psychological 8, 13
elderly 22
eugenic abortion 18
euthanasia
    administering 22, 28
    as murder 22, 23, 24, 33
    case studies 21, 29, 30, 37
    decriminalising 28
    guidelines 31
    in Britain 21, 22, 34
    mandatory 24
    passive 24
    statistics 21, 22, 27, 33, 34, 35
    voluntary 21, 24, 25, 26

freedom of choice 13, 24

government action 16, 22, 27, 35

handicapped children 4, 6, 7, 8, 11, 26
    Down's Syndrome 19, 20
    support 19
hospices 21, 23, 24, 25, 26, 28
human dignity 24, 26, 27
Human Rights Trust 28

illegal abortions 2, 11

laws on abortion 5, 11, 12, 17
    Abortion Act 5, 11
    Human Fertilisation and Embryology Act 11
laws on euthanasia 24, 27, 32
    Homicide Act 32
    Suicide Act 27, 32
lethal injection 21, 22
LIFE 5, 8, 9, 13, 14, 16, 18, 19, 39
life support 22

media coverage 9, 22, 29
medical advances 24
medical practitioners 3, 11, 12, 17, 21, 31
    opinions 21, 23
mercy-killing 25, 28, 32, 34
miscarriage 8, 13
moral issues 11, 22
mortality rates 3, 8

National Abortion Campaign 6, 10, 12, 16, 17, 39
National Health Service 5, 11, 12, 17, 21
Netherlands 2, 3, 21, 27, 29, 31
Northern Ireland 12

pain/suffering 25, 28, 30, 31
palliative care 24, 26
Post Abortion Syndrome 5
pregnancy
    unplanned 13
    unwanted 4, 5
Pro-Choice Alliance 11, 39
pro-life 4, 5
    extremists 15
public opinion 4, 27, 33, 34

quality of life 4, 37

rape/incest cases 4, 12, 14
religion, on abortion 1, 5, 10
    Biblical passages 10
    Christian
        Orthodox 10
        Protestant 10
        Roman Catholic 10
religion, on euthanasia 24, 27, 34
respect for life/self worth 5, 23
rights 19, 25, 33
    aged 24, 33
    baby 6
    child 5, 7
    disabled 18, 19
    foetus 6
    women 1, 4, 13, 14
right to die 24

Society for the Protection of the Unborn Child (SPUC) 4, 39
Support Around Termination for Abnormality (SAFTA) 19, 20, 39
support available
    case study 20
    counselling 14, 19
    Helpline 19
    services 3

terminal illness 23, 24, 27, 28, 33
terminating pregnancy 1, 17
The Last Right 27

United States 5, 9, 15, 21, 22, 27, 34
    Death With Dignity Act 22

violence 14, 15
Voluntary Euthanasia Society 24, 26, 27, 30, 32, 34, 35

women
    choice 13
    consent 12
    equality 14
    health 39
    maternal suicide 9
    rights 1, 4, 13, 14

Yours 21, 33, 34

ADDITIONAL RESOURCES

You might like to contact the following organisations for further information. Due to the increasing cost of postage, many organisations cannot respond to inquiries unless they receive a stamped, addressed envelope.

Abortion Law Reform Association (ALRA)
27 - 35 Mortimer Street
London W1N 7RJ
Tel: 0171 637 7264

Alert
27 Walpole Street
London SW3 4QS
Tel: 0171 730 2800

British Pregnancy Advice Service
7 Belgrave Road
London SW1
Tel: 0171 828 2484

Brook Advisory Centres
153a East Street
London SE17 2SD
Tel: 0171 708 1234

Family Planning Association
27-35 Mortimer Street
London W1N 7RJ
Tel: 0171 636 7866

Human Rights Society
Mariners Hard
Cley
Holt
Norfolk NR25 7RX
Tel: 01263 740404

International Planned Parenthood Federation (IPPF)
Regent's College
Inner Circle
Regent's Park
London NW1 4NS
Tel: 0171 486 0741
Fax: 0171 487 7950

Libertarian Alliance
25 Chapter Chambers
Esterbrook Street
London SW1P 4NN
Tel: 0171 821 5502
Fax: 0171 834 2031

LIFE - Save the Unborn Child
LIFE House
Newbold Terrace
Leamington Spa
Warwickshire
CV32 4EA
Tel: 01926 421587 / 311 667
Fax: 01926 336497

Lifeline Pregnancy Care
Cae Bach
4 Pant y Wennol
Llandudno
Gwynedd LL30 3DS
Tel: 01492 543741

National Abortion Campaign
The Print House
18 Ashwin Street
London E8 3DL
Tel: 0171 923 4976

Mary Stopes International
68 Grafton Way
London W1P 5LE
Tel: 0171 388 3034

National Child Birth Trust
Alexandra House
Oldham Terrace
London W3 6NH
Tel: 0181 992 8637 X25

Newlife
Kay House
51 Stonebridge Drive
Frome
Somerset BA11 2TW
Tel: 01373 451632

Peace Ethics Animals and Consistent Human Rights (PEACH)
88 Cobden Street
Luton
Bedfordshire LU2 0NG
Tel: 01582 459943

Pro-Choice Alliance
27 - 35 Mortimer Street
London W1N 7RJ
Tel: 0171 636 4619

Society for the Protection of the Unborn Child (SPUC)
7 Tufton Street
London SW1P 3QN
Tel: 0171 222 5845

Support after Termination for Abnormality (SAFTA)
73 -75 Charlotte Street
London W1P 1LB
Tel: 0171 631 0280

Voluntary Euthanasia Society
13 Prince of Wales Terrace
London W8 pG
Tel: 0171 937 7770

Women's Health
52-54 Featherstone Street
London EC1Y 8RT
Tel: 0171 251 6580

ACKNOWLEDGEMENTS

The publisher is grateful for permission to reproduce the following material

Chapter One: Abortion

Global overview of abortion, © International Planned Parenthood Federation (IPPF), *Abortions*, © Population Trends, Winter, 1994, *Life or death*, © Used with permission from Hayes Publishing Co, Author Dr. & Mrs. J.C Wilke, 1993, *The NHS and the pro-life hospital*, © The Guardian, 9th May 1994, page 11, *Questions you ask about abortion*, © National Abortion Campaign, November 1994, *Life*, © LIFE, 1993, *Abortion Statistics*, © National Abortion Campaign, January 1994, *Religious views on abortion*, © National Abortion Campaign, July 1991, *Abortion and the law*, © National Abortion Campaign, January 1994, *A woman's right to choose?*, © LIFE, February 1995, *It's murder out there*, © Ms London, January 1995, *Eight myths about abortion*, © National Abortion Campaign, November 1994, *Pre-birth screening*, © LIFE, February 1995, *Helping parents who discover their baby is abnormal*, © SATFA (Support Around Termination for Abnormality), January 1995.

Chapter Two: Euthanasia

Face up to the euthanasia debate, © The Observer, Sunday 4th December 1994, page 24, *Euthanasia: the dilemma of the decade*, © The Independent, 7th December 1994, page 23, *Euthanasia: the big debate*, © The Chronicle & Echo, 1st February 1995, *The case for legalisation*, © The Voluntary Euthanasia Society – EXIT, January 1995, *Human value or the scrapheap?*, © ALERT, February 1995, *The need for voluntary euthanasia*, © Voluntary Euthanasia Society, January, 1995, *The relief of pain*, © Human Rights, February 1995, *Dutch watch euthanasia on television*, © British Medical Journal (BMJ) Volume 309, 29 October 1994, *I sat holding his hand until he was dead*, © The Independent, 7th December, 1994, page 23, *His pain was too much for him to bear*, © The Independent, 7th December, 1994, page 23, *The Netherlands guidelines*, © The Voluntary Euthanasia Society, January 1995, *Current legislation*, © Voluntary Euthanasia Society – EXIT, January 1995, *Yes, help me to die*, © Yours Magazine, December 1994, page 6, *Scots support mercy killing*, © The Daily Record, December 1994, page 17, *Relatives keener on euthanasia than patients*, British Medical Journal, Volume 309, 29 October 1994, *Relative attitudes*, © The Guardian, February 1995, *'One in four' GPs get pleas for euthanasia*, 9th February, 1995, page 7, *Doctor euthanasia survey*, © Doctor, February 1995, *A flicker of hope*, © BEST Magazine, 27th September 1994, page 54.

Photographs and illustrations

Pages 1, 7, 10, 12: National Abortion Campaign, page 4: Joanne O'Brien / Format, pages 13, 30: K. Fleming / Folio Collective, pages 15, 37: A. Smith / Folio Collective, pages 17, 23: A. Haythornthwaite / Folio Collective, page 13, 14, 18: LIFE, page 20: Brenda Prince / Format, page 21: Ken Pyne.

Craig Donnellan
Cambridge
April, 1995